2023 CAPM Mock Practice Tests

Fully aligned with the Latest ECO Updates - Based on the PMBOK 7th Edition & the Agile Practice Guide

Yassine Tounsi

Introduction

These CAPM Mock Tests are fully aligned with the new January 2023 Certified Associate in Project Management (CAPM) Exam syllabus and reflect the 2022 ECO updates.

This book includes a total of **360 questions** based on the PMBOK 7th Edition, the Agile Practice Guide, as well as other recommended preparation resources included in PMI's Exam reference list.

To thoroughly prepare for the 2023 CAPM certification exam, this book offers you **4 Targeted Practice Tests**, each covering the new domains outlined in the updated 2022 CAPM ECO, in addition to **2 Full Mock Exams**, each includes 150 Highly realistic questions to simulate the real exam and help you test your understanding of project performance domains and approaches.

The book is structured according to the domains of the new ECO:

- Practice Test 1 = **Project Management Fundamentals & Core Concepts** (Domain 1)
- Practice Test 2 = **Predictive, Plan-Based Methodologies** (Domain 2)
- Practice Test 3 = **Agile Frameworks/Methodologies** (Domain 3)

- Practice Test 4 = **Business Analysis Frameworks** (Domain 4)
- Full Mock Exam 1
- Full Mock Exam 2

Each practice test comprises 15 questions including multiple-choice, multiple-selection, graphs, and fill-in-the-blanks, to perfectly reflect all types of questions that you will encounter in the 2023 CAPM exam.

Each Full Mock Exam includes 150 questions to help you simulate the whole exam experience, practice exam time management, and imitate the same exam conditions to minimize the stress and intimidation on the day of the exam.

This book involves challenging scenario-based questions, with detailed explanations, as well as corresponding references from **PMBOK 7th edition**, **The Agile Practice Guide**, as well as other recommended resources in the PMI's Exam Reference List.

Boost your confidence and proficiency before taking the CAPM certification exam using these practice tests to help you identify any knowledge gaps and clear any hard-to-understand concepts.

You can determine how prepared you are to take the CAPM exam based on your score on the Full Mock Exams:

- Less than 50%: You are not prepared enough. It's highly recommended to thoroughly go through your studying materials again.
- Between 50% and 60%: You are still not there yet. It's recommended that you concentrate on your knowledge gaps and retake your practice tests.
- Between 60% and 70%: You are almost there. If you still have time before the exam date, you can use it for more practice.
- Between 70% and 80%: You're prepared! You have a good chance now to pass the exam.
- More than 80%: You are perfectly prepared. With such a score, you're more likely to hit an Above target score in all domains!

PS: Please note that the singular pronoun "They", along with its inflected or derivative forms, them, their, theirs, and themselves, is often used in this book as a gender-neutral third-person pronoun.

For any questions or inquiries please visit:
www.yassinetounsi.com

Project Management Fundamentals & Core Concepts - Questions

Question 1

During product validation, a key stakeholder refuses to sign off the acceptance document, claiming that some of the functionalities do not meet their expectations. What should the project manager have done to avoid this situation?

    A. Involve the key stakeholder during the quality control phase

    B. Involve the key stakeholder during the project initiation phase

    C. Involve the key stakeholder during the planning phase

    D. Involve the key stakeholder during all project phases

Question 2

After being assigned by management to lead a new project, the project manager is immediately asked to develop the project charter in order to launch the project as soon as possible. To develop the project charter, the project manager will need the following documents: (Select three)

    A. Strategic plan

    B. Business case

    C. Agreements

    D. Project plan

Question 3

A project manager is assigned to a project consisting of four phases. Which of the following meetings should the project manager hold at each phase to ensure the continuous commitment of project stakeholders?

A. Kickoff meeting

B. Retrospective meeting

C. Risk review meeting

D. Stage gate meeting

Question 4

While managing an industrial project, a project manager notices that two stakeholders are always debating which may have a negative impact on the project. Which of the following options is used to document and monitor this type of situation?

A. Dispute log

B. Problem log

C. Change log

D. Issue log

Question 5

A project manager notices that his colleague, who is a fellow project manager, shows up at the office with new high-tech gadgets every day. This raises his suspicions that his colleague might be accepting gifts from hardware vendors who will be bidding on one of their company's upcoming multimillion-dollar contracts. Which of the following should the project manager do?

A. Warn the concerned colleague that such gifts aren't appropriate and leave it at that

B. Convince his colleague to return the items and stop accepting any gifts from vendors

C. Directly ask his colleague whether these items were gifts from vendors or he purchased them himself

D. Report his colleague to the organization so that a conflict-of-interest investigation can take place

Question 6

Constraints and assumptions are important for projects. They should be identified, controlled, and monitored continuously. Wrong assumptions or constraints can impact the project. For instance, when a constraint turns out to be wrong, it affects the project:

A. Positively

B. Negatively

C. Depends on the constraint

D. Depends on the project

Question 7

When the execution of a rebranding project was completed, several key stakeholders, including the sponsor, were reluctant to accept deliverables and close the project. What should the project manager do in this situation? (Select three)

A. Identify and resolve any open issues. Then, be firm on formal closure.

B. Formally close the project. Stakeholders will get well-acquainted with the new brand by that time.

C. Identify and openly discuss the reasons for reluctance.

D. Invite earnest feedback from all sides and try to identify any misunderstanding.

Question 8

All of the following statements are true, except:

A. A project can have several stakeholders

B. A program is a big project

C. Portfolio management is aligned with organizational strategy

D. Multiple projects can be aligned with one program

Question 9

A project manager is leading a hotel construction project in a foreign country where corruption is widely spread. After facing trouble obtaining the required construction permits from local authorities, a team member suggested giving a bribe to the local officials to get things going and execute the project without issues. How should the project manager react?

A. Refuse to give a bribe

B. Give the smallest amount of money possible

C. Negotiate a non-monetary bribe

D. Ask the team member to give the bribe on their behalf

Question 10

A project manager is working on a contract. Now that they completed their contract and closed the project, the project manager is out of work. What type of organizational structure does the project manager work in?

A. Strong matrix

B. Projectized

C. Functional

D. Weak matrix

Question 11

You are simultaneously managing six projects in the company. Two projects are of a similar type, while the other four are entirely different. You work as a _____.

A. Portfolio manager

B. Program manager

C. Project manager

D. Program coordinator

Question 12

During the kick-off meeting of their first project, the project manager presents the project plan to the attending stakeholders. When going through the details, the project manager notices that most stakeholders don't seem happy about the plan. A certain stakeholder even expressed their frustration with how inaccurate this plan describes their expectations. What is the most likely reason behind the project manager's inaccurate description of stakeholders' requirements?

A. The project manager did not use the project scope as a guide when creating the project plan

B. The project manager only presented the first draft of the project plan, so it can be always improved

C. The project manager did not engage the project stakeholders enough to be able to accurately capture their requirements

D. The project manager did not explain the project well enough. A better presentation of the plan would have prevented this misunderstanding

Question 13

A project manager was assigned to a park redevelopment project which consists of cleaning and equipping the park for local families and residents. The project involves a really big number of stakeholders since it includes multiple phases and different types of tasks to execute. What should the project manager do?

A. Disregard low-power stakeholders

B. Only engage the high-interest stakeholders

C. Analyze all stakeholders in order to prioritize engagement

D. Report the issue to the project sponsor

Question 14

During the planning phase, the project manager speculated that there will be no changes in the composition of the project steering committee. But, since any change could be very critical to the project, the project manager assigned a team member to monitor for triggers. Where should the name of the person responsible for monitoring the steering committee be recorded?

A. Risk register

B. Issue log

C. Change log

D. Stakeholder register

Question 15

Halfway through the project, the sponsor designates an inspector to check the quality of the deliverables so far. The project manager doesn't know the inspector in person, but they overheard that they are not flexible and working with them is usually hard. What is the best way for them to handle the situation?

A. Ask the sponsor to designate another inspector

B. Ignore the inspector's designation since they are an external stakeholder

C. Collaborate with the inspector and provide them assistance when needed

D. Use their soft skills to talk the inspector into looking past any quality issues and not reporting them to the sponsor

Project Management Fundamentals & Core Concepts - Answers

Question 1 = D
Explanation: Stakeholders need to get involved early on during project planning and sometimes during the project initiation as well. Key stakeholders should also be involved during the quality control phase so that they can assess the project deliverables and recommend any changes before the official acceptance. Since the concerned key stakeholder is responsible for signing off the acceptance document, their power is considered high. Therefore, stakeholders who are identified to have high power using the power/interest grid should be managed closely and/or kept satisfied throughout the whole project.

Question 2 = A, B, C
Explanation: To develop the Project Charter, the project manager needs business documents such as the project's business case, benefits/strategic plan, and agreements. The project plan is developed once the project charter is signed.

Question 3 = D
Explanation: Stage-gate or phase review meetings represent an opportunity for project stakeholders to review project progress along with planned future actions. In these meetings, project stakeholders can assess whether or not

the project is on track to meet the organization's expectations (PMBOK 7th edition, page 42). You should schedule gate meetings at key milestones throughout your project to not only ensure it is on track but also demonstrate to the project stakeholders that you are staying on course.

Question 4 = D

Explanation: The issue log, also called an issue register, is a project document that records and tracks all issues that have a negative impact on the project (PMBOK 7th edition, page 185). Once created, it'll be the project manager's tool to monitor and communicate all that is going on in the project. Such issues may involve resources leaving the project, conflicting teams, or even individuals with low morale. A change log is used to document all change requests. Problem log and dispute log are both made-up terms.

Question 5 = C

Explanation: The best way to act in this situation is to verify facts before taking any action. A violation based only on suspicion should not be reported. The project manager can get the facts right by telling his colleague that he is concerned about how things might appear and simply inquire about the source of the items. As a project manager, you should never jump to conclusions. You should always double-check facts before reporting a conflict-of-interest situation.

Question 6 = A
Explanation: Constraints are limitations imposed on a project, such as the scope, schedule, quality, budget, risks, or resources. If assumptions end up being false, it is bad news for the project. However, if constraints turn out to be false, it is a good thing, as it means that the project will be positively affected because constraints are limitations imposed on the project.

Question 7 = A, C, D
Explanation: The project manager should not close the project when key stakeholders are not satisfied. They should try to discuss, identify, and resolve any issues or misunderstandings first.

Question 8 = B
Explanation: Programs are not big projects. While a program mainly focuses on maximizing the organization's profits, project management targets the creation of deliverables that meet and satisfy stakeholder needs.

Question 9 = A
Explanation: Regardless of what may happen, the project manager should not offer a bribe. Instead, they should find a way to resolve the problem through legal procedures.

According to the PMI Code of ethics, the project manager should steer away from any illegal activity such as corruption, theft, embezzlement, fraud, or bribery.

Question 10 = B

Explanation: A Project-oriented organization, or a projectized organization, is one in which a considerable part of its processes and activities take place in the form of projects. There is no defined hierarchy; resources are brought together specifically for the purpose of a project. When a project is complete, they either get transitioned to another project or released.

Question 11 = A

Explanation: In portfolio management, a group of related or non-related programs and projects are managed in coordination (PMBOK 7th edition, page 244). Portfolio management is intended to reduce the gap between strategy and implementation by aligning projects to attain business objectives.

Question 12 = C

Explanation: Since requirements are not accurately defined and stakeholders are not satisfied, the project manager most likely didn't engage them sufficiently. Stakeholder engagement ensures a proactive identification of their needs and requirements, which can promote alignment and buy-in of the project. The project plan is derived from the scope. So, if the scope is not defined in collaboration with relevant stakeholders, the plan will most likely fail to meet their expectations. The stakeholders are unhappy with the plan content, not with the way it was presented. Since the project manager is presenting the plan during a kick-off meeting, we can conclude that the scenario involves a predictive project. Consequently, it's improbable that the project manager is presenting a draft to stakeholders since the purpose of a kick-off meeting is to present a final or properly elaborated version of the plan to get stakeholders' buy-in.

Question 13 = C

Explanation: As a project manager, you cannot leave out or disregard any stakeholders. Ignoring any of the project stakeholders can be very costly and can dramatically impact the project. You should identify all project stakeholders, regardless of their number, then analyze each one of them in order to prioritize the engagement. (The PMBOK Guide 7th Edition, page 12). Stakeholder engagement falls under the project manager's responsibilities, and should not be delegated to the sponsor.

Question 14 = A

Explanation: A risk register contains a list of all identified risks, their description, planned responses, probability, impact, risk owner, etc. (PMBOK 7th edition, page 185). In the described scenario, the change in the composition of the steering committee is considered a risk and the name of the person responsible for managing it should be noted in the risk register. Once the risk occurs, it becomes an issue. Since the described situation doesn't involve any issues yet, the issue log is not the correct answer. The situation doesn't involve any change requests either. Therefore, a change log is not the right option. The stakeholder register includes information about the project stakeholders and their classification. Unlike the stakeholder engagement plan, the stakeholder register doesn't contain action items for when, how, and who should monitor and engage stakeholders.

Question 15 = C

Explanation: When a new stakeholder is identified, they should be analyzed, prioritized, engaged, and then monitored (PMBOK 7th edition, page 12). In the described situation, the project manager should engage the inspector by collaborating with them. Regardless of the situation, stakeholders should never be ignored. On the other hand, it's not appropriate to ask the sponsor to replace the inspector without a solid reason. Plus, the project manager should certainly avoid influencing the inspector's work or decisions as it can undermine the project quality and lead to corruption.

Predictive, Plan-Based Methodologies - Questions

Question 1

When the dimensions of the dug canals for the new dam project were compared to the plan, a huge variance was revealed. Therefore, the project manager had to call for a meeting with the team to decide what to do next. In which of the following process groups does the project manager's activity take part?

- **A.** Executing
- **B.** Closing
- **C.** Monitoring and Controlling
- **D.** Inspecting

Question 2

After creating the network diagram, the project manager identified three critical paths. What should the project manager do next?

- **A.** Approve the network diagram and closely monitor all three critical paths
- **B.** Approve the network diagram and closely monitor the longest path among the three
- **C.** Re-examine the network diagram since it's supposed to only have one critical path
- **D.** Re-examine the network diagram since it's not supposed to have more than two critical paths

Question 3

After completing the creation of the scope statement, a project manager wanted to make sure that all of the project deliverables were identified and could be managed effectively. So, they opted for the _____ method to develop the WBS in order to capture all of the project's details.

    A. Scope decomposition

    B. Bottom-up estimating

    C. Rolling wave planning

    D. Checklist analysis

Question 4

During a project status meeting, the project manager updated the sponsor on the project performance by informing them that the SPI is 0.75 and the CPI is 1.05. What does this indicate?

    A. The project is over budget but on schedule

    B. The project is within budget but behind schedule

    C. The project is on schedule and within budget

    D. The project is behind schedule and over budget

Question 5

A project manager is managing a project that consists in implementing an accounting application for a pet store. During a project performance review meeting, they presented the following figures:

AC = $4,000, PV = $5,000, and EV = $5,500. What does that indicate about the project?

A. Since both the CV and SV are positive, the project is under budget and ahead of schedule

B. These numbers are insufficient to calculate the project SPI and CPI

C. Since the CV is negative, the project manager has probably spent more than they initially planned to

D. Since the SV is negative, the project is behind schedule

Question 6

Network diagrams are a visual display of project work as they show the connection between work activities and how they progress from the project's start to its completion. The longest path in a network diagram is known as:

A. Critical Path

B. Critical Chain

C. Float

D. Free Float

Question 7

A project manager is assigned to a 12-month project that has a $100,000 budget. Six months have passed and $60,000 has been spent. On closer inspection, the project manager finds out that so far, only 40% of the work has been completed. The value of the completed 40% work is referred to as:

A. Planned value

B. Earned value

C. Actual cost

D. Cost variance

Question 8

In a predictive approach, which of the following statements are true about project deliverables? (Select two)

A. Project deliverables should be identified throughout the project lifecycle

B. Project deliverables can be products, services, or any other type of outcome

C. Once project deliverables have been identified, they should not be changed anymore

D. The acceptance criteria for deliverables should be described in the project agreement

Question 9

Which of the following options represents the characteristics of the predictive project management approach? (Select two)

A. Scope, time, and cost are determined in the early phases of the project life cycle

B. Change is limited as much as possible during project execution

C. The scope is determined early in the project life cycle, but time and cost are routinely modified

D. After one iteration, deliverables have enough functionality to be considered complete

Question 10

Within the predictive approach, which of the following terms is used for both costs and schedules to establish what you'll measure against later in the monitoring and controlling phase?

A. Variance

B. Expected value

C. Baseline

D. Estimates

Question 11

The following diagram represents the decomposition of the project deliverables into smaller tasks. What is this diagram called?

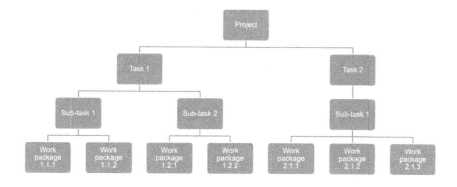

A. Affinity diagram

B. Product breakdown

C. Product roadmap

D. Work breakdown structure

Question 12

Prior to a meeting with the sponsor to update them on the project status, a project manager is going through the project status report which shows that the SPI is 0.8, while the CPI is 1.1. What should be more concerning to the project manager?

A. Nothing, the project is performing well

B. Cost

C. Schedule

D. Risk

Question 13

A project manager is managing a project with a distributed team, fixed budget, and tight deadlines. Knowing that they're adopting a predictive approach, what should the project manager do to avoid any scope creep and keep their team focused on delivering a product that meets requirements?

A. Ask the project team to skip small requirements so that they can only focus on big and important ones

B. Ensure that all alterations to the scope are authorized through a formal process

C. Prevent stakeholders from directly interacting with the project team

D. Scope creep cannot be avoided in a predictive project, therefore the project manager should adopt an agile approach instead

Question 14

A project manager is leading a high-risk project that has recently suffered from fluctuating performance and a high defect rate. During a meeting, the sponsor asks for an overview of work performance and where the project is currently standing. Which of the following documents should the project manager send to the sponsor?

    A. Quality report

    B. Status report

    C. Risk report

    D. Project management plan

Question 15

Before taking a long leave, a project manager informed the person filling in for them that they should regularly calculate the project's Earned Value (EV). Among the following options, what is the right description of an Earned Value?

    A. The difference between the budgeted cost of the performed work and its actual cost

    B. The value of the labor that has been employed on the project date

C. The method of determining how much of the budget should have been spent based on the amount of work accomplished to date

D. The amount of money that has been spent so far on the project

Predictive, Plan-Based Methodologies - Answers

Question 1 = C

Explanation: Reviewing the project performance in comparison to plans is part of the monitoring and controlling process group. These processes are meant for tracking, adjusting, and reporting on the project performance, as well as implementing corrective actions when needed to ensure the project is on track, budget and time-wise. Inspecting is not a process group, it's rather a risk identification activity.

Question 2 = A

Explanation: The project manager should approve the network diagram and closely monitor all three critical paths. Theoretically, there is no limit on how many critical paths a network diagram could have. If a project has more than one critical path, then all critical paths must have exactly the same length.

Question 3 = A

Explanation: Scope decomposition is a planning method used to decompose and subdivide the project and scope deliverables into more manageable, small work units. The decomposition level depends on the complexity and size of the project (PMBOK 7th edition, page 84).

Question 4 = B

Explanation: A Schedule Performance Index (SPI) of less than 1 indicates that the project is behind schedule. A Cost Performance Index (CPI) greater than 1 means that the project is within the predetermined budget.

Question 5 = A

Explanation: Since SV = EV − PV and CV = EV − AC then SV = $5,500 − $5,000 = $500 and CV = $5,500 − $4,000 = $1,500.

The Cost Variance (CV) is positive, which means that the project is under budget, and since the Schedule Variance (SV) is positive too, that means the project is also ahead of schedule.

Question 6 = A

Explanation: In a network diagram, the critical path is the path with the longest series of tasks (PMBOK 7th edition, page 238). Activities that are not on the critical path have some float (also called slack) that allows some margin for delay without causing the delay or change of the project end date. Free float is the amount of time an activity can be delayed without delaying the early start of the immediate subsequent activity. The critical chain is also the longest path in the network diagram, but unlike the critical path, it takes into consideration resource availability in addition to technical dependencies.

Question 7 = B

Explanation: Earned Value refers to the value of the work accomplished to date (PMBOK 7th edition, page 239). If the project gets terminated at this point, Earned Value will show you the value that the project has produced. In this case, the project's Earned Value (EV) is $40,000 = 40% of the value of total work. The amount of $60,000 represents the Actual Cost (AC). The planned value is $50,000 (50% of the budget), while the cost variance is -$20,000 (EV - AC).

Question 8 = B, D

Explanation: Project deliverables can be products, services, or any other type of outcome. In a predictive approach, project deliverables should be determined, described, and agreed upon as early as possible in the project, to avoid any costly changes later on. Acceptance criteria should also be described and agreed upon. The change is possible and should follow the change request process.

Question 9 = A, B

Explanation: Predictive methods focus on thoroughly analyzing and planning the future while taking into account known risks. The scope, time, and cost are all predetermined early in the project life cycle. Predictive teams often establish a Change Control Board (CCB) to ensure that only valuable changes are considered for implementation.

Question 10 = C

Explanation: Cost and schedule baselines are used to assess performance in the monitoring and controlling phases.

Question 11 = D

Explanation: The WBS is a hierarchical decomposition of the total scope of work to create the required deliverables (PMBOK 7th edition, page 81). The planned work is included in the lowest level of the WBS components, which are called work packages. Product breakdown is a product analysis technique (PMBOK 6th edition, page 153). The product roadmap demonstrates the anticipated sequence of deliverables throughout the project duration. Affinity diagrams classify a large number of ideas into groups for analysis and review.

Question 12 = C

Explanation: Since the Schedule Performance Index (SPI) is less than 1.0, then the project is behind schedule. Consequently, the project manager should be concerned about the project schedule. Since CPI is 1.1, then the project is under budget. Thus, the project is on track cost-wise. There is no indication in the question that the project manager should be concerned about risks.

Question 13 = B

Explanation: The project manager can avoid scope creep by adhering to the agreed-upon change management process. Change management processes have to be set up front and should be very straightforward. Essentially, when a change is suggested, it should be reviewed, approved or rejected, and then incorporated into the project plan if it's approved (PMBOK 7th edition, page 87). Requirements shouldn't be skipped, small or big. Often, it's not appropriate to prevent the stakeholders from communicating with the project team. Not all projects are fit for the agile approach, therefore it's not appropriate to change the project's development approach just to prevent scope creep.

Question 14 = B

Explanation: The status report is a work performance report that includes information on the project's progress and status (PMBOK 7th edition, page 190). Even though the project is at high risk and is encountering quality issues, the sponsor didn't explicitly request a detailed risk or quality report. The sponsor asked for work performance information to help them gain insight into the project situation and make better decisions. A status report can include information about Earned Value (EV), trend lines and forecasts, reserve burndown charts, defect and risk summaries, etc. The project management plan is not a reporting document; it's a planning document that is elaborated in the project planning phase.

Question 15 = C

Explanation: Earned Value (EV) is the method used to measure how much of the allocated budget should have been spent in view of the work realized to date (PMBOK 7th edition, page 239). This technique allows the project manager to calculate the Cost Variance (CV), which is the difference between the budgeted cost of the performed work (EV) and its actual cost, to eventually find out whether the project is under or over budget. The amount of money that has been spent so far represents the Actual Cost (AC).

Agile Frameworks/Methodologies - Questions

Question 1

Drag the following terms to the right position in the Agile triangle of constraints below: Cost, Scope, Flexible, Fixed

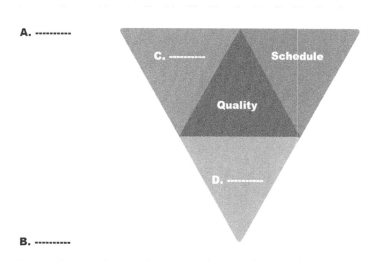

Question 2

An organization decided to use the agile approach for its new project. What should they get at the end of the first sprint?

    A. A plan for the subsequent sprint

    B. A potentially releasable product increment

    C. A Minimum Viable Product (MVP)

    D. A Work Breakdown Structure (WBS)

Question 3

In projects following the Scrum framework, which of the following questions won't be asked to team members during daily stand-ups?

- **A.** What have you completed since the last stand-up?
- **B.** What will you complete until the next stand-up?
- **C.** What do we need to finish as a team?
- **D.** Are there any impediments?

Question 4

A project manager is leading a web project using an adaptive approach. The project consists of creating an automatic notification system that alerts users when their cloud expenses exceed a predefined threshold. The project manager and the project team are currently preparing and updating user stories for the next iterations. What activity does this depict?

- **A.** Backlog refinement
- **B.** Schedule management
- **C.** Project management
- **D.** Sprint Review

Question 5

A project manager is facilitating a meeting attended by his project team as well as key stakeholders to prioritize all product backlog items according to their business value and risk level. Drag and drop each category of items in the right placement in the product backlog:

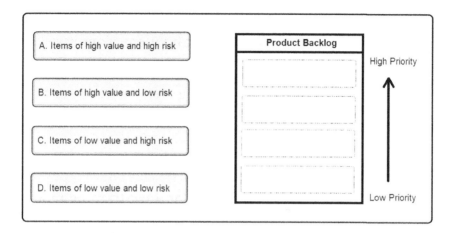

Question 6

A PMO is shifting from a predictive to an adaptive approach for delivering the organization's projects. For this purpose, concerned employees are undergoing agile training. During one of the training sessions, a participant wonders how many people a project team should include. What is the appropriate answer to the participant's question?

    A. 1 to 5

    B. 3 to 9

    C. 10 to 15

    D. There is no standard number

Question 7

A project manager is in the stage of selecting a development approach for a new project. Which of the following reasons will encourage the project manager to choose an adaptive approach over a predictive one?

   A. Change requests go through the organization's change control process

   B. Change requests are used for frequent planning

   C. Change requests are automatically approved

   D. Change requests are implemented as soon as they have been received

Question 8

A scrum master works on a project for a pet training mobile app. During the last retrospective meeting, several topics were evoked. Which of the following topics can be discussed in such a meeting?

   A. The feature of tracking a pet's activities

   B. Which tasks should be prioritized in the next sprint

   C. How to fix the regression of the chat feature

   D. Whether the standup timing is suitable for all team members

Question 9

An organization hires an external agile coach as part of its transformation project. In their final report, the agile coach mentions that measures should be taken to enable agile teams to be cross-functional. What does a cross-functional team mean?

   A. Individuals who collectively determine the best way to accomplish the goal of the sprint

B. Individuals who take part in guiding the product direction

C. Individuals who possess the necessary skills to produce a functioning product

D. Individuals who are in charge of authorizing and releasing work assignments

Question 10

During a workshop about the Agile approach, the project manager stated that Agile teams should be cross-functional and self-organizing, explaining that:

A. Each member of the team should be cross-functional and self-organized

B. The Agile team should have all the required skills to deliver the product on their own

C. The Agile team should have complementary skill sets and be able to organize the backlog by themselves

D. The Agile team should self-organize to acquire the necessary skills to be cross-functional

Question 11

This is the first time the project manager adopts the scrum framework for the project execution. One of the team members asks the project manager when a Sprint is considered completed. What should be the project manager's response?

A. When all product backlog items are completed

B. When all the tasks in the sprint are completed

C. When the sprint's defined timebox ends

D. When all product backlog items meet the Definition of Done (DoD)

Question 12

Using an Agile approach, where should product requirements be documented?

A. In the requirements log

B. In the product backlog

C. In the team charter

D. In the WBS

Question 13

An experienced scrum master is often asked "How long should a sprint be?" to which they always respond by saying "It depends, you should initially find a balance that works for the team, but typically an agile scrum sprint is _____ long."

A. 3-5 days

B. 1 week

C. 2-4 weeks

D. 5-8 weeks

Question 14

No matter what type of project they are managing or what type of challenges they might face, an agile project manager should make sure that the cross-functional team is always focused on:

A. Delivering frequently

B. Planning accurately

C. Improving quality

D. Delivering value

Question 15

A project manager needs to choose the suitable project management approach for the project they're leading. There are a variety of approaches to choose from, each ideally suited for a specific project type. Agile and Scrum are two of the most common and often conflated terms. Given their similarities, they can get confusing sometimes, but they are, in fact, two distinct concepts. What is the primary distinction between Scrum and Agile?

A. Agile is a set of values and principles, while Scrum only presents a set of values.

B. Agile is a set of values, principles, and practices, while Scrum only involves a set of values and principles.

C. Agile is a set of values and principles, while Scrum represents a set of values, principles, and practices.

D. Agile is a framework, while Scrum is a philosophy.

Agile Frameworks/Methodologies - Answers

Question 1

Explanation: Unlike predictive approaches, projects that follow adaptive approaches have a fixed cost and schedule, and flexible scope. A. Fixed, B. Flexible, C. Cost, and D. Scope.

Question 2 = B

Explanation: Agile uses iterations, also known as sprints, in each, a potentially shippable increment of the product is produced (Agile Practice Guide, page 101). The plan for the subsequent sprint is the output of the sprint planning event. A Minimum Viable Product (MVP) is a primary version of the product with just the basic functionalities with the purpose of collecting feedback or validating the product idea. It could take several sprints for the product to reach the MVP stage. Finally, a WBS is a planning technique used in the predictive approach.

Question 3 = C

Explanation: In contrast with flow-based Agile which focuses on the team's throughput, iteration-based Agile focuses on accountability through three standard questions:

- What was completed yesterday?

- What will be completed today?
- Are there any blockers or impediments?

Question 4 = A

Explanation: Backlog refinement involves preparing the next iteration's stories. In order to make sure the backlog contains the right items for the next iteration, the project manager, along with the team, should review and prioritize backlog items, ensuring that top items are ready to be delivered (PMBOK 7th edition, page 235). This activity can take place as a formal planned meeting or as a regular ongoing task.

Question 5

Explanation: Items of high priority and high risk should be on top as completing them sooner generates more new knowledge, which eliminates uncertainty and reduces risk. Items of high value and low risk should be tackled next. These items are great for achieving quick wins. The project team can then consider working on low-value and low-risk items. Finally, items of low value and high risk should be put off and placed at the bottom of the product backlog since they are not worth the effort. To sum up, the right order is: A, B, D, and then C from top to bottom.

Question 6 = B

Explanation: It's recommended that an agile team should include 3 to 9 members. Since the level of communication deteriorates as the team size increases, Agile organizations favor smaller teams. For instance, it's better to have two teams of five people than one team of ten.

Question 7 = B

Explanation: Unlike the predictive approach which requires change requests to go through the organization's change control process, the adaptive approach welcomes changes and uses them for frequent planning. During each iteration, the team focuses on producing a subset of the product's features, while continuously refining and reprioritizing the product backlog items to meet new or modified requirements. This means that change requests are not automatically approved; instead, they are discussed with the product owner first, and then they get prioritized in subsequent iterations as per their recommendations.

Question 8 = D

Explanation: During the sprint retrospective, the scrum master should identify what went well during the sprint and what can be done differently in the next sprint. A possible topic is the timing of the standup. If team members are showing dissatisfaction with the current schedule, then the retrospective meeting is the right event to discuss the issue. Backlog refinement meetings should address topics like the feature of tracking a pet's activities or how to fix the regression of the chat feature. On the other hand, the sprint planning meeting is the right meeting for discussing which tasks should be prioritized in the next sprint.

Question 9 = C

Explanation: A cross-functional team must possess the necessary competencies for creating a product or a service independently, without relying on other members outside of the team. On the other hand, a self-organizing team is when individuals collectively determine the best way to accomplish the sprint goal.

Question 10 = B

Explanation: A cross-functional team is a group of individuals who acquire different substantial skill sets that are enough to accomplish their common goal proficiently. A self-organizing team is autonomous in the sense that it does not rely on any outsiders to figure out how to best accomplish its work. This does not mean that each team member possesses all of the necessary skills for delivering the product; rather, they just need to be competent in their area of expertise.

Question 11 = C

Explanation: A sprint is considered complete only when it reaches the end of its duration/timebox, which is usually 1 to 4 weeks. In some cases, the sprint ends without finishing all of the assigned tasks, so this can't be the criteria for sprint completion.

Question 12 = B

Explanation: Product requirements are documented under the backlog as user stories. The backlog user stories are then continuously prioritized and refined. The WBS is only used in the predictive approach.

Question 13 = C

Explanation: A Sprint has to be long enough for the team to finish all included stories. As per a Scrum rule, a Sprint should never exceed one month. The duration of a sprint depends on the project size and complexity as well as the team's capacities. It takes 2 to 4 weeks on average to complete a sprint with a team of 3-9 members working on a single project.

Question 14 = D

Explanation: Delivering value should always be the agile team's top priority as it represents one of the agile manifesto principles: "working software over comprehensive documentation". From the client's perspective, value represents the benefit derived from using a product or a service.

Question 15 = C

Explanation: On the surface, Agile and Scrum look similar as they both rely on an iterative process, frequent client interaction, and collaborative decision-making. The primary distinction between Agile and Scrum is that Agile is a project management philosophy that utilizes a core set of values or principles, while Scrum is a specific Agile practice used to facilitate a project. Although Scrum is an approach within Agile, Agile does not necessarily imply Scrum since Agile encompasses a wide range of approaches. Scrum is based on a small set of core values, principles, and practices (collectively forming the Scrum framework). References: Agile Alliance & Essential Scrum by Rubin, Kenneth S (Preface).

Business Analysis Frameworks - Questions

Question 1

The project sponsor informed the project manager that they have doubts about whether the resulting product will satisfy business demands. Therefore, they are looking to keep costs to a minimum. What should the project manager do?

- **A.** Identify and implement the requirements for making a Minimum Viable Product (MVP)
- **B.** Gather all requirements and execute the project using an incremental approach
- **C.** Exclude certain stakeholders from the scope definition process in order to limit requirements
- **D.** Sign with the sponsor a fixed cost contract in order to limit project costs

Question 2

A project manager is examining the investment efficiency of two potential projects. Knowing that the discount rate is unknown, what should the project manager do?

- **A.** Select the project with the highest ROI
- **B.** Select the project with the lowest ROI
- **C.** Select the project with the highest NPV
- **D.** Select the project with the lowest NPV

Question 3

An organization is deliberating over two potential projects that have exactly the same payback period. After doing a benefit measurement analysis, the project manager finds out that project A has a lower Internal Rate of Return (IRR) than project B. What project should the organization choose?

A. Project A

B. Project B

C. There is no difference

D. The available information is not enough to make a decision

Question 4

A project manager receives a document from the customer containing the new project's requirements. When going through the document, the project manager finds it difficult to understand certain requirements, outputs, and most importantly the project's ultimate goal. What should the project manager do next?

A. Ask the customer for clarifications

B. Reject the new project as it involves a lot of ambiguity

C. Start planning the first iteration

D. Acquire a team to help analyze the project requirements

Question 5

To guide the development team on what they intend to achieve, a product owner of an HR solution shares the following table depicting the key deliverables of each quarter of the 9-month project. What agile artifact does this table represent?

Q1 2021	Q2 2021	Q3 2021
Web App User management Payroll module	Android App Reporting module Dashboard	iOS App Leaves module

A. Product vision statement
B. Product wireframe
C. Product roadmap
D. Product backlog

Question 6

The role of the product owner in an Agile project is:

A. Coordinating the work of the sprint and running the team

B. Having a vested interest in the project and its outcomes and interfacing with stakeholders

C. Representing the business unit, customer, or end-user

D. Completing the backlog items and signing up tasks based on established priorities

Question 7

The team of a predictive project discovers that many implemented features are different from the outlined scope in the scope statement. Which of the following documents should the project manager refer to in order to deal with this matter?

A. WBS

B. WBS dictionary

C. Requirements traceability matrix

D. Project charter

Question 8

A project manager is facing some struggles after joining a new company; her superiors noticed that during a kick-off meeting, she had difficulty answering questions about how the project fits in with the organization's objectives. What critical skill is the project manager lacking?

A. Business acumen

B. Ways of working

C. Communication skills

D. Power skills

Question 9

A project manager is leading a project that has become so large (multiple teams, long duration, and huge budget) that the sponsor has been replaced by a steering committee.

What should the project manager do to accommodate this new change?

A. Acknowledge that the stakeholders' structure has changed and tailor communication accordingly

B. Work according to the original plan while keeping in mind that the project may now include additional stakeholders

C. Hold a meeting with the new steering committee and continue working on the project

D. Share an updated status report with the new steering committee

Question 10

An organization assigned a new project manager to replace the one who recently left. What should the new project manager do first?

A. Consult the issues log and the lessons learned register to check if there is any serious problem

B. Consult the project charter to understand the project goals and its business case

C. Consult the project management plan to learn about the project baselines

D. Consult the stakeholders register to start interacting with the different parties involved in the project

Question 11

A project manager is assigned to manage a software development project. When they came across one of the project's key stakeholders in the company's hallway, the project manager seized the opportunity to get their feedback. The key stakeholder was impressed with the project's progress and requested that the project manager urgently add a new user story for marketing the product. How should the project manager respond to this request?

A. Welcome the stakeholder's request and add the user story to the sprint backlog

B. Add the user story to the product backlog and schedule it for the next sprint to protect the team from disruptions

C. Add the user story to the product backlog and let the product owner decide its priority

D. Refuse to create the user story since it's the product owner's responsibility to maintain and refine the product backlog

Question 12

All stakeholders are in a meeting to discuss a new project that is expected to start within one month and to last at least 10 iterations. One of the stakeholders mentions that someone should take the responsibility of developing and maintaining the product roadmap. Who should take this responsibility?

A. Project Manager

B. Development Team

C. Scrum Master

D. Product Owner

Question 13

A project manager is assigned to a hotel interior design project. One month into the project, the sponsor contacts the project manager to express his dissatisfaction with the deliverables, claiming that they match neither his requirements nor his expectations. How should the project manager react?

A. Continue working on the next deliverable as they need to finish the project on time

B. Talk to their manager to discuss the sponsor's concerns

C. Ensure that the next deliverables have enough features to meet the client's expectations

D. Perform a scope control to verify if the deliverables meet the project objectives

Question 14

A project manager is leading a project of gaming equipment development. The project team holds a monthly status review meeting with the product owner to review post-iteration deliverables. What's the best communication type to use in a status review meeting?

A. Push

B. Pull

C. Interactive

D. Formal

Question 15

To see where each team member stands regarding a certain decision, a project manager uses the Fist of five voting technique. When the team starts voting, one member holds up five fingers. What does it mean?

A. They want to intervene in order to further discuss the decision

B. They are totally against the decision

C. They totally support the decision

D. They want to refrain from taking part in the voting

Business Analysis Frameworks - Answers

Question 1 = A

Explanation: The Minimum Viable Product (MVP) is used to define the scope of the first release by identifying the requirements that would deliver value to customers (PMBOK 7th edition, page 243). An incremental approach is not suitable for the described scenario since the client won't get a usable product until the end of the project. It's not appropriate to exclude certain stakeholders in order to limit requirements. The project manager should involve all stakeholders in the process of collecting and prioritizing product features. Finally, a fixed-cost contract will not solve the problem in the described scenario since the main concern of the sponsor is verifying the product's business demand.

Question 2 = A

Explanation: Calculating a project's Net Present Value (NPV) requires knowing its discount rate (i):

Net Present Value (NPV) = Future payment (F) / [(1 + Discount rate (i)) ^ number of periods in the future the cash flow is (n)]. Since this is not an option in the described scenario, the project manager should rely on the Return On Investment (ROI) and pick the project with the highest value.

Question 3 = B

Explanation: The Internal Rate of Return is the annual rate of growth a project is expected to generate. The higher the IRR, the more desirable an investment is. Project B has a higher IRR, thus it will obviously be selected over Project A.

Question 4 = A

Explanation: In case of ambiguity, the project manager should first ask for clarifications from the customer before making any further decisions. The project involves unclear requirements and objectives. Thus, it's not appropriate to start planning project work or acquire a team without first creating a clear vision of what the project consists of.

Question 5 = C

Explanation: The product roadmap is built by the product owner to demonstrate the anticipated sequence of deliverables over the project duration (Agile Practice Guide, page 52). As an Agile artifact, the product roadmap sets the product's strategic view, indicating where the product is headed in both the short and long terms. In agile organizations, the product roadmap serves as a guide rather than a project plan. The product roadmap is different from the product backlog in that the product roadmap provides the big picture while the product backlog tackles the practical and feasible steps required to tangibly create the product. The Product wireframe is a mockup or a sketch of the user interface, high-level functionality, page layout, etc. A product vision statement outlines what a product would look like to ultimately achieve its vision and give purpose to its existence. A vision statement should be short, simple, and specific.

Question 6 = C

Explanation: The product owner represents the business unit, customer, or end-user as they're regarded as the voice of the customer. The Product Owner is responsible for maximizing the value produced by the team and ensuring that the stories meet the user's needs and comply with the Definition of Done (DoD) (PMBOK 7th edition, page 245). Apart from the project team, the product owner has significant relationships and obligations, including working with upper management, end-users, and other stakeholders.

Question 7 = C

Explanation: The traceability Matrix is a document that maps requirements as well as other aspects of the project. It's used as evidence to confirm that requirements have been fulfilled, as it typically documents those requirements along with issues and test results (PMBOK 7th edition, page 189).

Question 8 = A

Explanation: The PMI Talent Triangle is made up of three types of skill sets: Ways of Working, Power Skills, and Business Acumen. A project manager possessing business acumen skills should be able to explain the business value of their project and how it aligns with the organization's goals.

Question 9 = A

Explanation: On large projects, one sponsor might not be enough. A Steering Committee is established when a large project involves multiple business units, organizations, or individuals who all have a substantial stake in the project's success and outcomes. The project manager needs to be proactive and respond to this change. The initial communication plan for a single sponsor may not work for a steering committee. In order to ensure effective communication with the committee, the project manager must understand their communication requirements and preferences.

Question 10 = B

Explanation: First and foremost, the project manager has to understand why the project is being created in the first place; aka its business case. Moreover, the project manager should be aware of the project's predefined goals. These two elements along with the main deliverables are all defined in the project charter.

Question 11 = C

Explanation: The project manager should add the user story to the product backlog and let the product owner decide its priority. When a new requirement is received, it should be added to the product backlog (not the sprint backlog) and then prioritized by the product owner in order to be implemented. It is the responsibility of the product owner to maintain and refine the product backlog. This being said, a request can be made by any stakeholder and a user story can be created by anyone involved in the project and not just the product owner.

Question 12 = D

Explanation: In agile, the product owner should be in charge of managing the product roadmap since they are responsible for the product's success. The Product Owner's primary responsibility is to represent the business, which involves the creation and maintenance of the Product Vision and Roadmap, as well as the Product Backlog.

Question 13 = D

Explanation: Project scope verification or control involves reviewing deliverables to make sure that each is appropriately completed as per requirements. Any discovered inconsistency or dissimilarity should be rectified before seeking the sponsor's formal approval through the "validate scope" process.

Question 14 = C

Explanation: When an immediate response is required and the information you're communicating is sensitive and could be misinterpreted, you should use interactive communication. It involves one or more people sharing thoughts and ideas, with participants responding in real time. Interactive communication can take place through teleconferences or face-to-face contact. When using communication media such as emails, the project manager can't pick up on stakeholders' facial expressions and body language.

Question 15 = C

Explanation: The Fist of five or Fist to five is a voting technique that agile teams use to help them achieve consensus during decision-making meetings or sessions. This method is used as follows: The facilitator states the decision or action the team is going to vote on and then asks each one of the attendees to hold up a number of fingers that corresponds to their level of support for the stated decision. A closed fist signifies full objection whereas five fingers mean full support for the decision. Until everyone holds up three or more fingers, the voting goes through multiple rounds to achieve consensus.

Full Mock Exam 1 - Questions

Question 1

In an interior design project for a library, the client asks the team to increase the number of bookshelves beyond what was agreed on. Since the project is on schedule and adding additional shelves will make no difference, the project manager consents to the client's request. This is an example of:

- **A.** Gold Plating
- **B.** Customer Obsession
- **C.** Scope Creep
- **D.** Successful Project

Question 2

A project manager is assigned to her first project. The project manager implemented the project management plan meticulously but she was struggling with leading the project team effectively. Talking to her mentor, the project manager was advised to further focus on developing her leadership skills. In this situation, leadership means:

- **A.** Growing an ongoing business over a long period of time
- **B.** Ensuring predictability in an uncertain environment
- **C.** Adhering to standards and procedures
- **D.** Motivating people by establishing and maintaining vision

Question 3

A project manager is assigned to lead a new project that requires applying a hybrid development approach. Therefore, management enrolled the project manager in a training to help them learn how to combine agile principles with predictive techniques. Which aspect of the PMI talent triangle does this training target?

A. Business Acumen

B. Power Skills

C. Working Methods

D. Ways of thinking

Question 4

The stakeholder engagement process involves five steps. Add the following steps to the figure below: Identify, Monitor, Engage, and Understand & analyze.

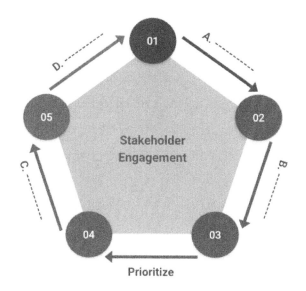

Question 5

After a long wait, a project manager gets a phone call from the project sponsor confirming that the budget has been allocated therefore the project can get started. The sponsor also informs the project manager that the project development approach should be defined as soon as possible and that the kick-off meeting should take place within the next two weeks. The project manager replies by saying that he must first receive the project charter. What is the purpose of a project charter?

A. To document the project approach

B. To formally authorize the project and document its initial requirements

C. To be used as a reference during the project kick-off meeting

D. To set up the project code of conduct

Question 6

Before announcing the completion of the project execution, the project manager of a construction project reviews deliverables and performs a site walkthrough. What is the project manager performing in this scenario?

A. An inspection

B. A handing over

C. An audit

D. A scope validation

Question 7

In a project context, guidelines and policies are classified as:

A. Regulations

B. Best practices

C. Assumptions

D. Constraints

Question 8

A project manager is in the stage of selecting a development approach for a new project. Which of the following reasons will encourage the project manager to choose an adaptive approach over a predictive one?

A. Change requests go through the organization's change control process

B. Change requests are used for frequent planning

C. Change requests are automatically approved

D. Change requests are implemented as soon as they have been received

Question 9

A project manager works for an organization that is used to the predictive approach. The organization's decision-makers attended a conference about Agile and decided to adopt this approach in their upcoming projects. The project manager got worried about losing their job because as far as they know, an Agile team is composed of team members, a scrum master, and a product owner. Thus, the organization will not need a project manager anymore. Is the project manager's concern justified?

A. Yes, the agile team doesn't include a project manager

B. Yes, the project manager should either convert to a scrum master role or look for a new opportunity in an organization following the predictive approach

C. No, the project manager can work as a product owner since both roles are similar

D. No, they can continue working as a project manager but they will be more of a facilitator

Question 10

A project involves dozens of stakeholders. Most of them need high-level information and updates about the project status, while the rest need more detailed information and frequent updates. To respond to these different requirements, what should the project manager create?

A. Power/interest grid

B. Salience Model

C. Stakeholder engagement plan

D. Stakeholder engagement assessment matrix

Question 11

A project manager is assigned to a farm fencing project of 300 ft. Since they have already managed two similar projects in another region, the project manager knows that a chain-link fence costs $10 per foot for materials, and between $10 and $15 per linear foot for labor, depending on the workers' experience and common rates in the region. What is the best way to estimate the labor cost per linear foot?

A. Three-point estimation

B. Parametric estimating

C. Bottom-up estimating

D. Analogous estimating

Question 12

After facing multiple quality issues, the project manager decided to identify top-priority defects by applying the 80/20 rule (aka the Pareto Chart). What should the project manager do next?

A. Find out the impact of each quality issue

B. Find out the frequency of each quality issue

C. Find out the urgency of each quality issue

D. Find out the cause of each quality issue

Question 13

A project manager was assigned to a large project that has unclear requirements and deliverables. After choosing an agile approach to deal with the situation, what should the project manager do next?

A. Acquire an agile coach to clarify the project scope

B. Facilitate the identification and prioritization of current work items, then ensure their execution in an iterative and incremental way

C. Set up a cross-functional team to help define all the needed iterations for completing the project

D. Have a meeting with the product owner or sponsor to discuss project baselines

Question 14

A project manager who follows the servant leadership style is onboarding a new team member who they believe can help fill skill-level gaps in the current project team. The project manager provides the new team member with a copy of the project charter and commits to sending them a copy of _____, which addresses team values, ground rules, and working agreements.

A. The employment contract

B. The resource management plan

C. The communication management plan

D. The team charter

Question 15

A project has been hampered by many quality issues, putting the project at risk. Which meeting should the project manager conduct with the team to figure out how to avoid or deal with such problems in the future?

A. Kick-off

B. Lessons learned

C. Risk review

D. Team building

Question 16

During the project planning phase, stakeholders insisted that their conflicting requirements should all be considered and consolidated. That made it hard for the project manager to create a plan that satisfies all stakeholders. What should the project manager do to establish a common ground?

    A. Build focus groups involving concerned stakeholders to discuss and resolve conflicting interests.

    B. Create a document explaining their personal point of view and ask conflicting stakeholders to review it.

    C. Give each stakeholder the opportunity to write a statement of work, and then merge all documents to create the project scope statement.

    D. Use their authorization and position as the project manager to decide which requirements should be prioritized.

Question 17

Regardless of the type of development approach that a project manager adopts for their project, their top priority should always be:

    A. Up-to-date documentation

    B. Efficient collaboration and strong relationships with all project stakeholders

    C. Satisfying customers by fulfilling project requirements

    D. Elaborating a robust plan and responding to change requests

Question 18

One year into managing a predictive project, and during the completion and closure process, the project manager faces a key stakeholder's refusal to sign off the deliverables due to non-compliance claims. What can the project manager do to ensure stakeholder acceptance?

    A. Issue a change request

    B. Conduct a sprint retrospective

    C. Change the SOW

    D. Conduct a variance analysis

Question 19

In a projectized organization structure, after getting the client's approval of deliverables and officially closing the project, what should be the project manager's next step?

    A. Perform a final quality inspection

    B. Inform the functional manager so they can assign the team to another project

    C. Check for any pending or incomplete tasks

    D. Release the project team

Question 20

A project manager keeps receiving negative feedback concerning one of the project suppliers. The conflicts between the project team and the supplier's team are getting worse recently and are starting to have a negative impact on the project. What should the project manager do next?

A. Send an email to the supplier's team manager explaining the alarming situation

B. Meet with the supplier's team manager to discuss the issue

C. Call the supplier's team manager and urge them to commit to the procurement agreement

D. Proceed with Alternative Dispute Resolution (ADR)

Question 21

A product owner selected a number of user stories with a total of 110 points for the next release. Knowing that the team's velocity is 20 story points, what's the estimated duration to complete the release?

A. 5 sprints

B. 5.5 sprints

C. 6 sprints

D. It's not possible to calculate the estimated number of sprints to complete a release in Agile

Question 22

An organization in need of accounting software conducts a make-or-buy analysis. The organization decides to go for in-house development since the analysis shows a payback period of fewer than 3 years. However, when acquiring resources, the project manager finds out that the developer's rate included in the make-or-buy analysis is only half the current rate in the market. What should the project manager do first?

A. Submit a change request

B. Inform the sponsor about their findings

C. Nothing; as long as the project's SPI and CPI are on track, this shouldn't be a problem

D. Update the make or buy analysis report

Question 23

Which of the below statements represents the most accurate definition of backlog refinement? (Select three)

A. The process of creating the initial list of product requirements, formerly known as backlog grooming.

B. When the product owner or team members review the backlog to make sure it has the proper items

C. The continuous elaboration of project requirements to satisfy the stakeholders' needs

D. The continuous activity of writing, updating, and prioritizing requirements

Question 24

A company must select one of two projects that have the same budget, but different returns and risk levels. Which tool or technique should be used in order to make the right decision?

A. Decision tree

B. Tornado diagram

C. SWOT Analysis

D. Sensitivity analysis

Question 25

In an effort to increase agile knowledge, a project manager has been paired with other Agile project managers to observe how they lead their teams. The project manager notices that many project decisions are the responsibility of the project team, while project managers are more facilitative than authoritative as they share a common vision and allow the team to focus on their work. What leadership approach does this depict?

A. Participative leadership

B. Autocratic leadership

C. Transformational leadership

D. Servant leadership

Question 26

A project manager has been assigned to a project in Japan. When meeting with the local project stakeholders, the project manager was offered a welcome gift since it's a local tradition to present gifts to guests when meeting them for the first time. What should the project manager do about it?

A. They should not accept the gift at any cost

B. They should accept the gift and inform management

C. They should accept the gift and keep the incident to themselves

D. They should accept the gift and politely return it later

Question 27

Working with the predictive approach, which of the following is most true?

A. Lag can be determined by making a forward pass

B. Lag is the maximum amount of time a task can be delayed without delaying the early start of its successor

C. Lag is waiting time

D. Lag is the maximum amount of time a task can be delayed without delaying the whole project

Question 28

Before starting the project, and after identifying all of the individuals and groups involved or affected by the project, the project manager took a step further by classifying stakeholders according to their level of power, interest, and influence. This step is referred to as:

A. Stakeholder analysis

B. Stakeholder identification

C. Stakeholder monitoring

D. Stakeholder engagement

Question 29

A project manager is leading a software project using a predictive approach. During execution, a team member developed a new feature that caused regressions on the other features already used by the client. What should the project manager do? (Select three)

A. Submit a change request to fix the resulted regressions

B. Inform the concerned stakeholders about the regressions, their impact, and the proposed solutions

C. Set up a lessons learned meeting to avoid similar issues in the future

D. Since it's an internal problem, try to fix it without the customer's notice

Question 30

A project manager learns that they were not assigned the human resources they were promised during the planning phase. Instead, they got a team that did not have the required skills for executing the project work. Taking into consideration that they work in a weak matrix organization, what should the project manager do?

A. Issue a change request to get a more qualified team

B. Negotiate with the functional manager in order to obtain the required team members

C. Take the matter to the project sponsor

D. Use their legitimate power by informing the organization that they will not perform the project without the needed resources

Question 31

A product owner who's new to the agile approach created the following user story: "As a customer, I want a new functionality so that I can achieve a 50% increase in sales". The project manager found the user story to be deficient. So, they reached out to the product owner to explain to them that:

A. The user story should follow a common structure

B. The user story should be specific and testable

C. The user story should not include financial values

D. The user story should be time-bounded

Question 32

A product owner creates a release plan based on an estimated team velocity of 50 story points. However, in the first two sprints, the team achieved 37 and then 35 story points. What can the agile project manager do in this case? (Select two)

A. Inform the product owner that, based on available empirical data, the release plan could not be achieved

B. Use their leadership skills to motivate their team to reach the estimated velocity

C. Extend the duration of the sprint until completing 50 story points

D. Study with the product owner the possibility of adding more resources to the team

Question 33

An organization recently transitioned to the agile approach. However, project team members always wait for the project manager to assign them work. How can the project manager help their team be self-organized?

A. Take a few weeks off to force the team to act on their own

B. Mentor the team on how to make their own decisions

C. Ensure that the team includes different functional expertise

D. Support the team by removing encountered impediments

Question 34

Three manufacturing lines are producing 5 mm diameter cylindrical steel bars. In order to perform a quality inspection, the project manager takes 10 random bars from each line. The following are the inspection results in mm measurements. The results of Line 1 can be described as:

	Bar 1	Bar 2	Bar 3	Bar 4	Bar 5	Bar 6	Bar 7	Bar 8	Bar 9	Bar 10
Line 1	4.45	4.50	4.40	4.45	4.40	4.45	4.50	4.45	4.40	4.45
Line 2	5.10	5.15	4.90	4.90	4.85	4.95	5.05	5.00	5.00	5.10
Line 3	5.00	5.05	4.95	4.95	5.05	5.00	5.05	5.00	5.05	5.10

A. Accurate

B. Precise

C. Both accurate and precise

D. Neither accurate nor precise

Question 35

A project manager is evaluating a potential industrial project. To determine whether its anticipated financial gains will outweigh its present-day investment, the project manager uses the Net Present Value (NPV) as an effective tool to help her determine whether the project will be profitable or not. For instance, NPV > 0 means:

    A. The project will lose money

    B. The project will break even

    C. The project is profitable

    D. We can't know until the ROI is calculated

Question 36

An associate project manager found that working on their interpersonal skills helped them manage stakeholders more efficiently. Which of the following are examples of interpersonal skills? (Select three)

    A. Communication style assessment

    B. Political awareness

    C. Project management certification

    D. Cultural awareness

Question 37

A project's performance measurements are calculated based on the following information: EV = $2,000 and AC = $1,000. What is the status of the project?

A. The project is ahead of schedule

B. The project is behind schedule

C. The project is under budget

D. The project is over budget

Question 38

A project manager is developing the business case of a green transportation project. To do so, they decide to use the SWOT technique. How should the project manager apply this technique?

A. Follow a Plan-Do-Check-Act cycle (PDCA Cycle)

B. Assess the business model using expert judgment

C. Identify the project's strengths and weaknesses

D. Conduct a benefit/cost analysis

Question 39

A project manager is managing an agile project in which the product owner has a relatively low involvement. The project manager continuously reminds the product owner of their responsibilities and that they should, for instance, take care of sorting the product backlog items by placing:

A. The easiest items at the top

B. The less valuable items at the bottom

C. The most recent items at the top

D. The less clear items at the top

Question 40

A project manager is leading a complex project with a very demanding sponsor. The sponsor wants to stay on top of every project progress update as well as all planned subsequent work. What's the best way for the project manager to communicate with the sponsor?

A. Send a comprehensive monthly report detailing all project progress aspects regarding scope, schedule, cost, risks, etc.

B. Schedule a monthly face-to-face meeting to discuss the project status

C. Schedule a meeting once or twice a week and let the sponsor know that they can also attend daily standups

D. Schedule a fortnightly meeting and give the sponsor access to the project management software so they can check real-time updates concerning the project status

Question 41

An agile project manager is concerned about the amount of time their team spends on planning. Which of the following planning activities the team shouldn't be involved in?

A. Iteration planning

B. Daily planning

C. Release planning

D. Portfolio planning

Question 42

While working on identifying risks, a project manager noticed that there is a disagreement among team members concerning the appropriate way to execute an important work item. What can the project manager do to mitigate this risk?

A. Outsource the concerned work item

B. Enroll the team in a training about the technologies related to executing that work item

C. Let the team self-organize and figure out how to execute the work item

D. Escalate the issue to the functional manager

Question 43

Agile is not fit for all projects, despite all the advantages it can bring forth. Therefore, it's important to understand the drawbacks of this approach. Which of the options below represent the disadvantages of the Agile approach? (Select three)

A. Poor resource planning

B. Limited documentation

C. Self-organized teams

D. Fragmented output

Question 44

A project manager works for a big matrix-structured organization where communication channels are complex and cross-functional. On a daily basis, the project manager communicates with the executive team and reports back to the manager. What type of communication does this describe?

A. Horizontal communication

B. Vertical communication

C. Parallel communication

D. Triangular communication

Question 45

A project manager at Clinica Labs, a biopharmaceutical corporation, intends to talk to her manager about obtaining additional resources for complex activities that her team is unable to perform. These resources will roll off the project as soon as the activities are completed. Which of the following skills does the project manager need the most in this situation?

A. Planning skills to identify resource requirements

B. Interpersonal skills to convince her manager of her need for additional resources

C. Interviewing skills to hire the required resources

D. Technical skills to respond to the risk associated with adding more resources

Question 46

In order to respond to the rapidly changing business environment, an organization has decided to use adaptive methods. To adopt an agile mindset, the project team can use all of the following questions while developing the product, except

A. What work can be avoided to only focus on high-priority tasks?

B. How can the Agile team work in a predictable manner?

C. What work should be prioritized in order to obtain early feedback?

D. How can servant leadership help the achievement of project goals?

Question 47

Using a predictive approach, the project manager resorts to management reserves to handle which type of risk?

A. Unknown unknowns

B. Known unknowns

C. Business risks

D. Pure risks

Question 48

A project manager is managing an online e-learning platform. The project team is following the Scrum framework and every few weeks they release a new version that includes more features, user interface changes, bug fixes, security patches, etc. In order to avoid confusing users with the continuous changes, the project manager decides to make all release information accessible to the platform members under the "News" section on the website. What type of communication is the project manager intends to use?

A. Push communication

B. Interactive communication

C. Pull communication

D. Proactive communication

Question 49

A project manager attended a leadership training workshop. The trainer listed the characteristics of servant leaders, then mentioned some examples of a servant leader's behavioral traits, such as: (Select two)

A. Helping a team member write a professional email to a stakeholder in order to get key information

B. Rewarding high-performing employees in order to motivate them

C. Checking up on a team member to find out why they've suddenly become an introvert

D. Inspiring their team with success stories

Question 50

A project manager has just taken over an ongoing project for creating a newborns' essentials brand. Items made of fabric are manufactured by external vendors. To get to know all vendors involved in the project, the project manager should check out:

A. RFQs

B. Stakeholder register

C. Vendors' proposals

D. Stakeholder engagement plan

Question 51

Halfway through a sprint, the development team realized that they planned for more work than they could possibly complete. What should the project manager advise the development team to do next?

A. Ask the product owner to remove some work items from the sprint backlog

B. Collaborate with the product owner to reprioritize the product backlog items

C. Continue work and put off discussing this issue to the sprint retrospective

D. Inform the product owner during the sprint review that some features could not be completed

Question 52

A project manager is assigned to lead a megaproject that requires experts and resources from different countries. Unable to predict worldwide epidemics, the project team is worried about facing another event like CoronaVirus that might cause delays and cost overruns. What should the project manager do during the risk planning phase? (Select two)

A. Add the risk to the risk register

B. Perform a qualitative risk analysis

C. Add the risk to the issue log

D. Monitor the development of the risk

Question 53

During project execution, a team member reaches out to the project manager to inquire about the work they need to accomplish in this phase of the project. Which of these documents comprises thorough descriptions of work packages?

   A. WBS

   B. WBS Dictionary

   C. Activity List

   D. Scope management plan

Question 54

A project manager for Steel Foundations has been brought on to the project in the very early stages and has been asked to write its charter. Over the past week, the project manager met with a number of stakeholders, received their input, and is now ready to have the charter signed. Who is responsible for signing the project charter?

   A. Project Sponsor

   B. Senior Management

   C. Project Manager

   D. Project stakeholders

Question 55

Knowledge garnered through personal experience is the most difficult to express, articulate, or write down. This type of knowledge is known as:

   A. Explicit knowledge

B. Tacit knowledge

C. Tangible knowledge

D. Formal knowledge

Question 56

Conditions under which a project manager must work and which they cannot control are called Enterprise Environmental Factors (EEF). Which of the following is not considered an Enterprise Environmental Factor?

A. Organization culture

B. Market standards

C. Corporate knowledge base

D. Work authorization systems

Question 57

A PMP-certified team member is under investigation for violating the Code of Ethics and Professional Conduct. What should the project manager do?

A. Fully cooperate with the investigation

B. Tell the PMI investigator that it would be a conflict of interest for them to cooperate with the investigation since they are the person in question is part of their team

C. Tell the PMI investigator getting involved or cooperating would be harmful to the project

D. Cooperate with the PMI investigator by truthfully answering all of their questions, but refuse to give them any witness statements

Question 58

Due to high levels of uncertainty, the project manager opts for the rolling wave method for the project planning. How is this method useful in this case?

A. It will help the project manager determine which activities are more important to prioritize

B. It will help the project manager organize the project's activities and tasks

C. It will help the project manager determine the sequencing of a large number of activities

D. It will help the project manager reach the proper level of detail in each work package at the right time

Question 59

A project manager is leading a 3D modeling project of a castle that will be built near a river. Halfway through execution, the sponsor requests the termination of the project since a dam will be built nearby, making the castle's location not appealing anymore. What should the project manager do?

A. Terminate the project as per the sponsor's request

B. Proceed with claims administration

C. Try to directly negotiate the matter with the sponsor in order to convince them to allow the project continuation

D. Insist on delivering the project since the dam has no association or impact on it

Question 60

An agile project manager noticed that several stakeholders have lost interest in the project; they rarely provide inputs, give feedback, or attend meetings. What can the project manager do to resolve this problem? (Select two)

A. Send a reminder before each meeting

B. Inform stakeholders that they can provide their feedback anonymously

C. Value and show appreciation of everyone's ideas

D. Demonstrate the working increments

Question 61

After multiple negotiation sessions, all of the terms and details were agreed upon and the seller finally got the 18-month building project contract for $715,500. What type of contract is used in this scenario?

A. Time and Material

B. Fixed Price

C. Cost Reimbursable

D. Cost Plus Incentive

Question 62

Mid-sprint, the development team's work was disrupted by a sudden issue concerning a dysfunctioning software feature. During the following retrospective meeting, the project manager decides to use the Five Whys method in order to investigate the problem. Why did the project manager choose to use this specific technique?

A. To identify the five main factors that caused the issue

B. To identify the root cause of the issue

C. To identify the five members responsible for the issue

D. To identify the five steps to take to resolve the issue

Question 63

A project manager is leading a construction project. Throughout its execution, the project was influenced by both Enterprise Environmental Factors (EEFs) and Organizational Process Assets (OPAs). Match the following statements with the corresponding influence category:

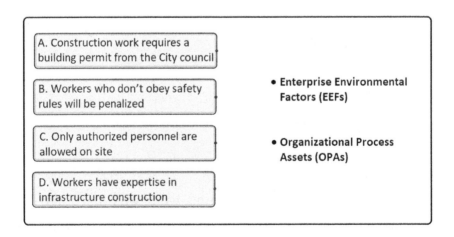

Question 64

When discussing their choice to opt for remote resources with the project sponsor, a project manager enumerated the many advantages of working with remote teams. They mentioned all of the following advantages, except:

A. Access to more skilled resources

B. Less travel and relocation expenses

C. Utilization of a war room

D. Reduction of time spent commuting

Question 65

A project manager has just joined a new organization. A majority of the organization's projects are conducted by experienced project managers. What should be the primary focus of the new project manager in order to ensure his efficiency?

A. Acquire a skillful team

B. Learn about the organization's culture

C. Get to know the organization's executive managers

D. Get to know the organization's project managers

Question 66

For a project in the robotics field, the project manager floated a tender for the high-tech equipment they needed. To clarify some points, the project manager held a bidder conference. Which steps did the project manager take during the bidder conference? (Select two)

A. Award the contract

B. Clarify any doubts

C. Explain the bid terms and conditions

D. Shortlist prospective sellers

Question 67

After 8 years of experience in the same position, a project manager gets promoted to a Portfolio manager role. A portfolio is:

A. A number of projects, programs, or operations that are all managed as a collection with the aim to achieve the organization's strategic goals

B. Analyzing IT requirements and ensuring regulatory requirements are followed

C. Following methods, processes, and tools to ensure that projects are managed as designed

D. Creates a common vision and helps senior management to see the potential strategic implications of corporate decisions

Question 68

A project manager canceled a Lessons learned review meeting due to time constraints. The potential consequences of this decision might implicate:

A. Issues faced through the project could reoccur due to the missed opportunity to identify preventive actions

B. Project management will get more difficult

C. Project cost will be greater

D. The project may not be accepted by the Project Management Office (PMO)

Question 69

The critical path method is a schedule network analysis technique. Which of the following statements is true regarding the critical path?

A. All of the tasks on the critical path should be critical themselves

B. If a task in the critical path is delayed, it will result in delaying the whole project completion date

C. A change request does not have any impact on the critical path

D. The critical path can be used in both predictive and adaptive life cycles

Question 70

After introducing a new foreign developer to the team, the project manager noticed that a certain senior team member seems to be avoiding any interaction with them. What should the project manager do about this issue?

A. Talk to the senior team member privately to try and find out the reason behind their behavior while making it clear that discrimination is neither tolerated nor accepted

B. Notify the functional manager of the senior team member's behavior and ask them to take the appropriate disciplinary action

C. Look past the senior team member's behavior since no conflict between the two has occurred and work seems to be going just fine

D. Address the issue in the next team meeting by scolding the senior team member and lecturing everyone about the importance of an inclusive work environment

Question 71

During the execution of a construction project, the supplier informed the project manager that delivering the new order of steel bars may have a 3-day delay. What should the project manager do next?

A. Negotiate the delay with the vendor to get it reduced

B. Look for another vendor

C. Evaluate the impact of the delay

D. Update the project schedule

Question 72

During project execution, the project team had an issue with an unreliable vendor. Since the incident had a high impact on the project scope, the project manager decided to terminate the vendor's contract and never deal with them again in the future. Where should the project manager record this issue?

A. Lessons learned register

B. Change log

C. Risk register

D. Issue log

Question 73

For a museum construction project, concrete is poured after the completion of rebar and formwork. Now, workers must wait 14 days before removing the formwork, as the concrete must be strong enough for this operation. The 14-day period is an example of:

A. A Lead

B. A Lag

C. Crashing

D. Fast-tracking

Question 74

A project manager is leading a predictive project. After identifying a risk, they decide to transfer it to another party by:

A. Buying insurance

B. Accepting a lower profit in case of cost overrun

C. Asking the sponsor to deal with the risk

D. Eliminating the risk through beta testing

Question 75

A project manager and their Agile team are demonstrating a potentially shippable product increment to the project stakeholders. What type of Agile meetings is the project manager conducting?

A. Review meeting

B. Standup meeting

C. Retrospective meeting

D. Deliverables meeting

Question 76

When the cost of quality of the project they're leading reached a certain level, the project manager was invited to a meeting with their line manager to explain the project situation. During the meeting, the project manager was asked about the project's cost of non-conformance. Which of the following fall under the cost of non-conformance? (Select three)

A. Rework

B. Scrap

C. Warranty work

D. Destructive testing loss

Question 77

A junior marketing consultant aspires to be a project manager. However, she often gets confused about what project management involves. To clear up the confusion, her mentor tells her that project management is:

A. An undertaken temporary endeavor to create a unique service, product, or result

B. The application of a set of knowledge, skills, tools, and techniques to project activities to meet the project requirements

C. The collection of programs that have been grouped to achieve strategic business goals

D. An organizational structure that aims to standardize project-related governance processes

Question 78

Foretheta is a Seattle-based IT company. Its latest project involves creating a mobile App for online training. The project manager decides to build a prototype for the App. What added value do prototypes provide? (Select two)

A. Allow for early feedback on the requirements

B. Reduce project cost

C. Allow the project to be completed faster

D. Help to address ambiguities

Question 79

Before a demonstration meeting with the client, a team member discovered a defective component that could be either repaired or replaced. The cost of both options is negligible, they're both risk-free, and the whole operation will require less than 1 hour. However, the team spent 15 minutes discussing the two options without reaching an agreement. What should the project manager do in this case?

A. Allow the discussion to continue until the team agrees on a solution

B. Set up and facilitate a formal meeting with their team members

C. Escalate the issue to the project sponsor

D. Call for a vote in order to reach a decision

Question 80

During the last three daily standup meetings with the team, the project manager notices that a new team member is struggling with one of their assigned tasks as they seem to be making no progress towards completing it. What should the project manager do?

A. Ask an experienced team member to take over the task

B. Check whether other team members can help their new colleague with the task after the standup meeting

C. Express their disappointment to the new team member and encourage them to make more effort

D. Ask the new team member to check the team ground rules

Question 81

After baselining the scope and during project execution, a key stakeholder, who is a member of the Change Control Board (CCB), requested a new service. Taking into consideration that the project manager is convinced that this new service can add value to the project, what should they do?

A. Implement the change request since the key stakeholder is a member of the CCB

B. Implement the change request since it will add value to the project

C. Submit a change request according to the change control system

D. Record the change request in the change log

Question 82

During the risk identification process, attrition of resources was identified as a major risk. As a response, the project manager decided to opt for financial incentives to motivate their team members. What type of risk response are they following?

A. Acceptance

B. Mitigation

C. Transference

D. Avoidance

Question 83

A project task is 90% complete. It cannot, however, be finished until another task is completed. What type of dependency is this? (Select two)

A. Finish-to-start (FS)

B. Finish-to-finish (FF)

C. Mandatory dependency

D. Discretionary dependency

Question 84

A project manager is submitting a number of potential projects to management for selection and approval. Since the organization is currently facing financial challenges, the project manager has been told that it cannot invest more than $350,000 per project, with a leeway of 5% on either side. The 5% leeway is part of:

    A. Organizational Process Assets (OPAs)

    B. Enterprise Environmental Factors (EEFs)

    C. Threats

    D. Risks

Question 85

A project manager is assigned to an accounting software development project. In its beta version, some users reported that the software freezes one to three times a day. Since the project manager needs more information to fix the problem, they asked the users to fill in a _____ whenever the issue occurs to include information about how the freezing happens and how long it lasts.

    A. Check sheet

    B. Cheat sheet

    C. Checklist

    D. Survey

Question 86

After purchasing a software for their project, a project manager identifies a potential risk; the bought version might be old. In case that risk occurs, the project manager will just need to go to the settings and update the software version. Therefore, the project manager decides to passively accept the risk. In this case, why is passive risk acceptance the appropriate approach?

A. Because the probability of risk occurrence is very low

B. Because the risk occurrence is difficult to identify

C. Because it's better to deal with trivial risks when they occur

D. Because the risk is not on the critical path

Question 87

In a weak matrix organization, employees work across multiple projects and with various departments within the company to increase employee interaction and promote teamwork spirit. In the event that additional employees are needed, who is in charge of the hiring process under this matrix?

A. The project manager

B. The sponsor

C. The project team

D. The functional manager

Question 88

Due to a financial crisis, an organization decided to pause all internal projects to an undefined date. Knowing that a project manager within this organization has a weekly meeting with a subcontractor who provides the majority of the project's physical resources, what is the best type of communication to inform this subcontractor of the contract discontinuation decision?

A. Informal written

B. Formal written

C. Informal verbal

D. Formal verbal

Question 89

A senior project manager joins an ongoing project following the resignation of its former project manager. What should the new project manager do first?

A. Review the project budget to determine if more funding is required

B. Go through the issue log to check the previous and current difficulties the project is facing

C. Examine the project charter to understand the project goals and deliverables

D. Add a new activity to the project schedule concerning knowledge transfer

Question 90

A project manager is leading a project within a functional organization. Halfway through the project implementation, a team member left the organization. What should the project manager do first?

A. Collaborate with the functional manager to get a replacement

B. Update the project's resource breakdown structure

C. Reassign their workload to the project team member

D. Evaluate the impact of the team member's departure on the project

Question 91

A solar-powered car project is almost finished when the project manager receives an approved change request to replace a defective component of the car batteries. What should the project manager do?

A. Record the problem in the issue log

B. Meet with the change control board to discuss the matter

C. Repair the defective component

D. Replace the defective component

Question 92

The following chart was presented during a retrospective meeting. Which of the following statements is true regarding this chart?

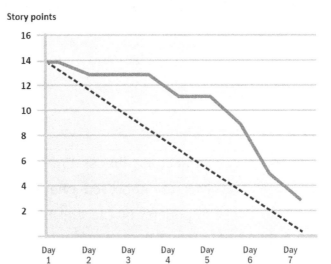

Story points

A. This burnup chart shows that there is work left at the end of the sprint

B. This burnup chart shows that the planned work is completed before the end of the sprint

C. This burndown chart shows that there is work left at the end of the sprint

D. This burndown chart shows that the planned work is completed before the end of the sprint

Question 93

A project manager is leading a new virtual reality game development project. The project is scheduled to last 10 months with a budget of $100,000. One month into the project, the team completed 10% of the total work. What is the project's current Schedule Performance Index (SPI)?

A. 0.1

B. 1

C. 1.1

D. 10

Question 94

In agile, what is the planning poker technique used for?

A. Estimating how much effort is needed to complete tasks

B. Estimating how much work is left in the sprint

C. Testing the project and identifying blockers

D. Measuring the sprint velocity

Question 95

A project manager is leading the construction project of a luxury residency. Before proceeding with the site excavation process, a government clearance must be issued. What kind of dependency does this describe?

A. Soft logic

B. Preferential logic

C. External dependency

D. Discretionary dependency

Question 96

During a meeting with 15 team members, the product owner was discussing and collecting ideas about the product requirements. Now, participants are in the last stage of selecting the final idea. However, since there were a lot of suggested ideas, they decided to vote. After voting, the product owner finds that a particular idea received 9 votes, so they go with that option. What type of decision-making does this depict?

A. Unanimity

B. Majority

C. Plurality

D. Dictatorship

Question 97

A senior software engineer has recently been assigned to manage a project using the Agile approach. To ensure that they successfully deliver the project, the project manager should first:

A. Identify all risks

B. Determine all of the sprints' activities

C. Define the project success criteria

D. Define quality metrics

Question 98

A project manager is assigned to a project that follows an adaptive approach. After gathering all requirements, the project manager previewed 3 to 5 releases to achieve the project goal. They intend to define the details of each release progressively when they get more insight and feedback from key stakeholders. What should the project manager do, taking into consideration that the project has a fixed budget that cannot be exceeded?

A. Since the budget is fixed, the project manager should adopt a predictive approach for the project instead of an adaptive approach

B. Since chances of scope creep are high, the project manager should ensure that a Change Control Board (CCB) is established before the start of the project

C. Before the start of the project, the project manager should set a fixed number of releases and develop a detailed budget for each of them

D. The project manager should work with stakeholders to prioritize work for each release until running out of budget

Question 99

A project manager depends on time-boxing to help team members avoid wasting time on shallow work and stay focused on the main deliverables. Which of the following statements best describes time-boxing?

A. Duration of intense activity within a specific release

B. A time frame for executing specific activities

C. Tight planning to reduce the time required for an activity completion

D. Setting a deadline for product delivery

Question 100

Even though they create an agenda and timebox for the meetings they're facilitating, the project manager can't seem to engage all attendees. What can they do to address this issue?

A. Make meetings shorter to prevent boredom

B. Limit the interventions of the most talkative attendees to allow others to participate

C. Change to remote meetings to make everyone feel more comfortable

D. Encourage all attendees to participate and share their thoughts by asking for their opinions on the discussed matters

Question 101

A project manager is wrapping up a one-year project. Which of the following activities should be prioritized?

A. Updating the change log

B. Releasing the project resources

C. Completing the knowledge transfer activities

D. Celebrating the project completion

Question 102

A project manager is facing some challenges because of a key stakeholder. The project manager collaborated with this stakeholder in previous projects where the latter frequently changed her requirements and created trouble whenever those requirements were not met. How should the project manager deal with this issue?

A. Adopt an Agile approach

B. Involve the concerned stakeholder right from the start

C. Ask the concerned stakeholder to mend her ways

D. Inform management about the issue

Question 103

Adopting a predictive approach to plan an agriculture project, a project manager chooses the _____ method to estimate the cost by using work breakdown.

    A. Analogous

    B. Parametric

    C. Top-down

    D. Bottom-up

Question 104

What is the difference between a corrective and a preventive action?

    A. Corrective actions address what will occur in the future, while preventive actions address what already occurred in the past

    B. Corrective actions address what already occurred in the past, while preventive actions address what will occur in the future

    C. Corrective actions are part of the executing process group whereas preventive actions are part of the controlling and monitoring process group

D. Preventive actions are part of the executing process group whereas corrective actions are part of the controlling and monitoring process group

Question 105

Knowledge is sometimes depicted as an iceberg since it involves two categories:

A. Explicit and Tacit

B. Known and Unknown

C. Direct and Indirect

D. Deep and Superficial

Question 106

From past experience, the project manager of a construction project knows that they might face the risk of not receiving the needed sand supply on time. Therefore, they included this potential threat in the risk management plan. If this risk were to occur, the project manager will have to purchase the sand from another supplier. But, in this case, there may be some differences in the sand quality, which would be a _____ risk.

A. Residual

B. Secondary

C. Compliance

D. Primary

Question 107

In order to ensure that the project is performed in accordance with the organization's requirements, the project manager carries out a tailoring process. Under this context, Tailoring is:

A. The knowledge and practices which are applicable to most projects in most cases

B. The application of a set of knowledge, skills, tools, and techniques to the project activities in order to meet its requirements

C. The selection of the appropriate processes, inputs, tools, techniques, and life cycle phases for managing a project

D. The application of knowledge, skills, tools, and techniques needed for meeting a program requirements

Question 108

A project manager works for an NGO, leading a campaign to collect medical supplies for refugees. While contacting pharmaceutical companies to convince them to take part in this campaign, they enumerate the many benefits this partnership can bring them. Which of the following are considered tangible benefits of participating in this campaign? (Select two)

A. Generating more revenue

B. Building a stronger brand since more people will know about them after the campaign

C. Building a good reputation

D. Benefiting from taxes reduction for supporting an NGO

Question 109

3 months into project execution, the sponsor gets into a financial crisis and asks the project manager to immediately end the project. What should the project manager do next?

A. Try to persuade the client to complete the project

B. Talk to their management about the situation

C. Start the close procurement process

D. Start the close project process

Question 110

A project manager is leading a team with distributed members across different countries. Apart from cultural barriers, the team seems disconnected, leading to multiple rework cases. What could the project manager do to improve communication within the team?

A. Collaborate with senior management to co-locate the team

B. Request from the team to only use emails for communication to avoid any misunderstanding or misinterpretation

C. Hold short daily meetings with all team members to sync on what's everyone is doing

D. Offer team members training about overcoming cultural barriers

Question 111

An organization asked the project manager to send a report on the cost of quality. The report stated that the total cost was $30,000, detailed as follows:

Item	Training	Rework	Inspection	Scrap	Warranty charges
Cost	$10,000	$10,000	$5,000	$3,000	$2,000

According to the above table, how much is the appraisal cost of the project?

    A. $2,000

    B. $3,000

    C. $5,000

    D. $10,000

Question 112

All of the following are either Agile or Lean frameworks except:

    A. Scrumban

    B. eXtreme Programming

    C. Waterfall

    D. Crystal Methods

Question 113

A project manager is leading a construction project. Work on light spots is pending since ceiling tiles are still being installed, which may cause some delays within the project. What should the project manager refer to in order to check the electricity team's availability in the next two weeks to resolve this dependency?

A. Resource Calendars

B. Responsibility Assignment Matrix (RAM)

C. RACI Matrix

D. Organigram

Question 114

While traditional project management follows predefined phases and sticks to the predetermined scope, Agile project management approaches:

A. Encapsulate analysis, design, implementation, and test within an iteration

B. Involve documenting, estimating, and sequencing each planned activity in detail

C. Use Gantt charts along with well-defined activities, responsibilities, and time frames

D. Map the iteration backlog into a Work Breakdown Structure (WBS)

Question 115

Grade and quality are two of the most commonly used terms in project management on a daily basis. Which of these statements is correct when talking about a performed service or a developed product?

A. Low quality is acceptable, but a low grade is not

B. A low grade is acceptable, but a low quality is not

C. Low grade and low quality are both unacceptable

D. Quality and grade are the same

Question 116

A project manager is assigned to lead a project abroad. At the start of the project execution, the project manager gets worried about the country's high levels of violence in public. The project manager gets approached by a local police officer who pledges to keep them and their team safe during their stay in return for a private money transfer. How should the project manager respond?

A. They should not pay the police officer and ignore this incident

B. They should not pay the police officer and rather follow the chain of command

C. They should pay the police officer and consider it as a facilitation payment

D. They should pay through a 3rd party considering how suspicious the situation is

Question 117

A project manager is attending a meeting to present her project to the company's committee for approval. The committee members, including senior managers and subject matter experts, are asking her tough and critical questions. Which project selection technique does this scenario describe?

- **A.** Brainstorming
- **B.** Scoring model
- **C.** Murder board
- **D.** Benefit analysis

Question 118

A project manager is leading a project using an adaptive approach. Halfway through the iteration, they realize that some user stories are unexpectedly delayed. Along with identifying any potential impediments, the project manager works on helping their team _____ Work In Progress (WIP).

- **A.** Increase
- **B.** Limit
- **C.** Compress
- **D.** Skip

Question 119

A Scrum Master attends or facilitates the different Scrum events including the Sprint, Sprint planning, Daily standup, Sprint review, and Sprint retrospective. Which of the following options describes the sprint retrospective meeting?

- **A.** A meeting for refining product backlog items

B. A meeting for discussing the negative and positive aspects of a sprint as well as any possible improvements

C. A meeting for defining and evaluating the work of the next sprint

D. A meeting held at the end of the project's last sprint

Question 120

An organization is making a progressive transition from the predictive to the adaptive approach. What can the project manager do to prepare their team for the transition? (Select two)

A. Provide training for the team on agile values and practices

B. Apply the "learning-by-doing" philosophy by immediately switching to agile approaches

C. Plan a gradual transition by introducing a few iterative or incremental techniques to their current project

D. Suggest a full transition since agile practices cannot be combined with predictive ones

Question 121

A project manager has made certain that all of the required tasks have been accomplished. However, upon an external post-completion audit, a significant penalty was imposed on the performing organization. What could the project manager have done differently to make sure that no liabilities arose following the audit?

A. Verify that all of the tasks indicated in the scope statement were completed

B. Verify that all identified defects were fixed

C. Ensure that all documents were updated before closing the project

D. Ensure that all closing formalities were followed as per the defined contractual procedures

Question 122

Throughout his long career, a project manager has always followed a servant leadership style, particularly with agile teams. What does servant leadership imply?

A. One individual in charge of directing and guiding the team

B. Carrying out work through iterations, with one prominent leader

C. Naming a team leader, while team members serve as followers

D. Understanding and addressing the needs of team members

Question 123

A project manager created the following high-level hierarchical list of human and physical resources of a project that consists in creating a bulk SMS platform for marketing campaigns. What does this visual illustration represent?

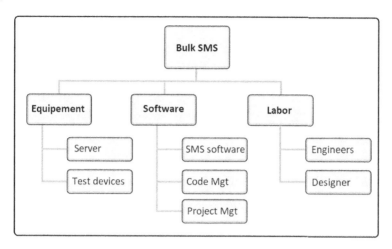

A. Resource calendar

B. Organization breakdown structure

C. Resource breakdown structure

D. RACI chart

Question 124

An organization is conducting several projects, each has its own due date. The available resources must be simultaneously assigned to different projects. Fearing that her project might face some delays, a project manager meets with the functional manager to discuss additional resource allocation to her project. Which of the following is probably the most important skill that the project manager will need for that?

A. Planning

B. Negotiating

C. Facilitating

D. Documenting

Question 125

Which of the following Scrum meetings is product-centered?

A. Daily standup

B. Sprint planning

C. Sprint review

D. Sprint retrospective

Question 126

A manufacturing company that operates according to the predictive approach, is launching a project to create an innovative product using new technology. The details of the components of work packages have been defined and constraints for each component have been identified. Top management requested a precise cost estimate of the project. What estimating technique should the project manager use?

A. Top-Down

B. Parametric

C. Bottom-up

D. Analogous

Question 127

A project manager was asked to lead a project of flight booking website development. The airline requested that the website should be able to support one thousand visitors per hour. This condition is also known as a(n): (Select two)

A. Requirement

B. Scope

C. Acceptance criterion

D. Deliverable

Question 128

A project manager is leading a project using a hybrid approach. Shortly after acquiring the resources, they discover that their team members are politically very engaged; almost all of their meetings end with a political dispute between team members. The project manager has decided to put an end to this before it deteriorates team members' relationships, by prohibiting any political discussions. Where should the project manager note this rule?

A. Team charter

B. Project charter

C. Resource charter

D. Resource management plan

Question 129

One of the project team's key members leaves the project for personal reasons. The project manager did not plan for such a scenario but they managed to get a replacement with the help of a staffing agency. However, they have to pay them a higher salary. This will result in extra costs which fall under the project's:

A. Contingency reserve

B. Cost

C. Management reserve

D. Budget

Question 130

A project manager was assigned to develop a mobile app with a team of five members. Which of the following project life cycles can be adopted by the project manager?

A. Initiation, planning, executing, monitoring and controlling, and closing

B. Wireframing, prototyping, designing, developing, testing, and deploying

C. Development, introduction, growth, maturity, and decline

D. Forming, storming, norming, performing, and adjourning

Question 131

Place the following project budget components in the right position in the figure below: Project budget, Cost baseline, Contingency reserve, and Management reserve.

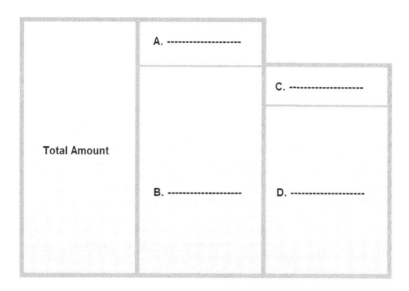

Total Amount

A. --------------------

B. --------------------

C. --------------------

D. --------------------

Question 132

In order to handle high levels of change and ensure the active participation of all interested parties, a project manager adopts a change-driven project development approach, which is also known as:

A. Adaptive approach

B. Predictive approach

C. Waterfall approach

D. Hybrid approach

Question 133

A project manager is assigned to lead a construction project for the first time. Three months in, the project manager notices that the running cost is higher than expected. So, they decide to assess the project's financial status by calculating the difference between Earned Value (EV) and Actual Cost (AC). What is the project manager calculating?

A. Cost Performance Index

B. Cost Variance

C. Planned Value

D. To-Complete Performance Index

Question 134

An experienced project manager believes that managers should embrace transparency in their projects, as its many benefits often outweigh its disadvantages. However, the project manager thinks that, while it is favorable to share many aspects with the project team, there are a few things that shouldn't be shared with everyone. As a project manager, you must be transparent about:

A. Confidential information

B. Proprietary information

C. Unproven information and gossip

D. Her decision-making processes

Question 135

At the beginning of the project planning phase, the project manager would always emphasize how important it is for all data to be precise and accurate. During a meeting, a team member asks if there is really a difference between precision and accuracy. How should the project manager reply?

A. Precision and accuracy are mutually exclusive

B. Accuracy measures exactness while precision measures correctness

C. Accuracy measures correctness while precision measures exactness

D. Precision and accuracy are actually the same

Question 136

A project manager is leading the construction of a new bridge in their city. In order to track the project's progress, the project manager sets milestones in the project schedule. What is the typical duration of a milestone?

A. Half of the project duration

B. The same duration as the project life cycle

C. Zero

D. One month

Question 137

In order to gather end-user feedback, a senior project manager of an Enterprise Resource Planning (ERP) project discusses several ideas with the project team and then they draw the following diagram. What tool are they using?

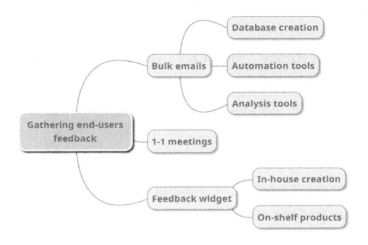

A. Mind map

B. Affinity diagram

C. Decision tree

D. Data representation

Question 138

An agile coach has been hired by an organization to help them implement the Scrum framework. One of the team members asked them who should prioritize items in the sprint backlog. What should be the agile coach's response?

A. The Scrum Master

B. The Product Owner

C. The cross-functional team members

D. All of the above

Question 139

A project manager is leading a project using an adaptive development approach. How should the project manager plan the project activities?

A. Plan all of the iterations work before the start of the project

B. Progressively elaborate the scope based on continuous feedback

C. Develop a high-level plan as the project progresses

D. Execute the project activities described in the Statement Of Work (SOW)

Question 140

When an agile team was discussing the technical choices of their new project during the zero sprint, a senior team member recalled a similar past project that went through some big challenges and ended up being over budget and behind schedule. What should the project manager do next?

A. Look for the performance details of the mentioned past project in the Organizational Process Assets (OPAs)

B. Look for the performance details of the mentioned past project in the Enterprise Environmental Factors (EEF)

C. Look for the performance details of the mentioned past project in the issue log

D. Since the mentioned past project followed a predictive approach, its performance details are irrelevant

Question 141

A project manager closed all contracts related to their construction project, except one that concerns setting up security cameras. The only thing left for this contract is to go through a quick inspection by an expert in order to check out wireless connection, night vision, cloud storage, etc. Knowing that the security cameras are working fine and that the project needs to be closed as soon as possible, what should the project manager do?

    A. Close the contract and the project with no inspection

    B. Close the contract, but keep the project open

    C. Close the project, but keep the contract open

    D. Keep the contract and the project open

Question 142

A project manager has been assigned to an agile project that is already mid-execution. Which of the following should the project manager check to examine the high-level description of the project scope?

    A. Project charter

    B. User stories

    C. Epics

    D. Work breakdown structure

Question 143

A predefined budget allocation is a project _____.

- **A.** Budget
- **B.** Assumption
- **C.** Risk
- **D.** Constraint

Question 144

A project manager at Max Data has just put the finishing touches on her final project report before meeting with her manager. She spent the last few weeks holding numerous lessons-learned sessions to get feedback from project participants for the final report. For what reasons did the project manager hold lessons learned sessions? (Select three)

- **A.** Lessons learned databases are an important element of the organizational process assets
- **B.** Lessons learned meetings focus on identifying individuals accountable for failures and errors
- **C.** Lessons learned meetings include recommendations for future performance improvements
- **D.** Phase-end lessons learned workshops represent a good team-building exercise for project members

Question 145

At the end of the project, and during the lessons learned meeting, a project manager presents the following chart, stating that project expenditures over time form a(n) _____.

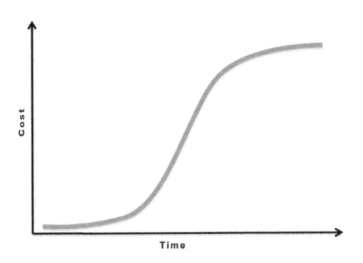

A. Slanted line

B. S curve

C. Z curve

D. Integral curve

Question 146

A project manager facilitates a meeting attended by project stakeholders to discuss a recurring issue with one of the project vendors. As a facilitator, the project manager should: (Select two)

    A. Be in full control of the discussion and its outcomes

    B. Be responsible for taking meeting notes

    C. Help stakeholders find a common ground and solve the issue

D. Provide guidance without interfering

Question 147

After releasing the product, the organization faced poor quality claims from the customer. What kind of non-conformance costs the organization might incur?

A. Internal costs

B. Appraisal costs

C. External costs

D. Risks and issue response costs

Question 148

Which is the most important characteristic of an Agile team?

A. Their ability to create and manage their own work schedule

B. Their ability to be flexible and adaptable

C. Their ability to accurately plan the project

D. Their ability to simultaneously work on their tasks

Question 149

A project manager is leading a project using the predictive approach within a functional organization. During the project execution, the project manager encountered an issue that was not identified in the planning phase. To resolve this issue, additional work should be added to the project scope, which will result in an increase in the project cost. To whom should the project manager escalate the need for additional funds to complete this work?

A. Program manager

B. Product owner

C. Project sponsor

D. Functional manager

Question 150

In the project initiation phase, the sponsor asked the project manager to provide an approximate cost estimate for the project by the end of the day. What should the project manager do in this situation?

A. Create the product backlog items, estimate how many iterations are required to complete the items, then sum up the cost estimate of each iteration

B. Create the WBS and sum up the cost estimate of each work package

C. Create the cost management plan

D. Provide an estimate based on similar past projects

Full Mock Exam 1 - Answers

Question 1 = C

Explanation: Scope creep (also known as "feature creep" or "requirement creep") refers to the uncontrolled expansion of the project's scope (PMBOK 7th edition, page 249). Customer obsession consists of an excessive focus on providing a better customer experience by meeting and even exceeding your client's needs. However, customer obsession shouldn't mean delivering beyond scope since the latter can increase the project schedule and cost, thus decreasing the success rate of the project. The tackled situation is not considered gold plating since the client is the one who brought up the change request; it was neither the project manager nor team members who added changes without the client's approval, as gold plating implies.

Question 2 = D

Explanation: Successful leaders are able to communicate the project vision to their team so that everyone has a shared vision of the bigger picture. When the whole project team understands this vision, individuals are able to see where they fit in and how each of them contributes to the success of the project (PMBOK 7th edition, pages 23-25).

Question 3 = C

Explanation: Working Methods (also known as Ways of Working) are the skills that the project manager is developing through the training. The other two aspects of the PMI talent triangle are Power Skills and Business Acumen. Ways of Thinking is a made-up term.

Question 4
Explanation:
A. Identify B. Understand & analyze C. Engage D. Monitor (PMBOK 7th edition, page 10). Stakeholders' engagement starts by identifying all parties directly or indirectly connected or involved in the project. Next, the identified stakeholders must be fully understood in terms of their beliefs, attitudes, expectations, etc. towards the project in order to be able to analyze each one's level of power, interest, impact, etc., and prioritize them accordingly. After that, an engagement plan is created according to the findings of the previous steps, where a project manager should ensure clear and constant communication, the satisfaction of stakeholders' requirements and expectations, and issues resolving when needed. Monitoring stakeholders is the final step in the process, and it entails monitoring any changes in their attitudes or power levels to adapt the engagement plan accordingly.

Question 5 = B
Explanation: A project charter is used to formally authorize both the project manager to start the project, as well as document the project's objectives and its high-level scope. It

also defines the responsibilities and roles of all involved parties in the project (PMBOK 7th edition, page 184).

Question 6 = A

Explanation: During an inspection, the project manager reviews deliverables and performs a site walkthrough if applicable. Audits, on the other hand, are carried out to determine if project activities comply with organizational and project policies, processes, and procedures (PMBOK 6th edition, page 294). In other words, audits are performed on processes while inspections are performed on products. The project manager here is neither validating the scope with the customer nor handing over deliverables to them.

Question 7 = D

Explanation: Project constraints are restrictions that limit the project in a certain way. A cost restriction, for instance, means that the project is limited by its allocated budget or resources. Other constraints include policies, standards, guidelines, etc.

Question 8 = B

Explanation: Unlike the predictive approach which requires change requests to go through the organization's change control process, the adaptive approach welcomes changes and uses them for frequent planning. During each iteration, the team focuses on producing a subset of the product's features, while continuously refining and reprioritizing the product backlog items to meet new or modified requirements. This means that change requests are not automatically approved; instead, they are discussed with the product owner first, and then they get prioritized in subsequent iterations as per their recommendations.

Question 9 = D

Explanation: In Agile, there are three common roles: cross-functional team members, product owner, and team facilitator. The team facilitator can also be called project manager, scrum master, project team lead, or team coach. A team facilitator's role is to remove impediments, facilitate, and coach the team. In other terms, the team facilitator should have strong servant leadership skills (Agile Practice Guide, pages 40-41).

Question 10 = C

Explanation: A stakeholder engagement plan sets up strategies and actions to ensure the positive and effective involvement of all stakeholders in the project (PMBOK 7th edition, page 187). The power/interest grid, Salience Model, and stakeholder engagement assessment matrix are tools and techniques to analyze stakeholders and assess their level of engagement. Unlike the stakeholder engagement plan, these tools do not generate or comprise practical information on how to engage and monitor stakeholders such as the frequency of official meetings, recipients of status reports, communication channels, etc.

Question 11 = A

Explanation: The three-point estimating is the triangular distribution of pessimistic, optimistic, and most likely estimates. This technique is used when there is insufficient historical data or when there is only judgmental data. Since the two similar projects were performed in another region, the project manager can't precisely define the labor cost using analogous estimating. Parametric estimating can be used to estimate the cost of the 300 ft fence after figuring out the labor cost per linear foot. Plus, bottom-up estimating can't be used in this situation since the labor cost depends on the workers' experience and the applied rates in the region, not on the volume and decomposition of the required work.

Question 12 = B

Explanation: A Pareto diagram is a histogram that ranks issues from the ones with the highest frequency to the ones with the lowest frequency. The diagram is created according to Pareto's Law, which states that 80 percent of the problems come from 20 percent of the issues (also known as the 80/20 rule).

Question 13 = B

Explanation: The project manager should start by facilitating the identification and prioritization of evident requirements, hence helping with the elaboration of the product backlog. Next, and since the project is following an agile approach, the project manager should execute work iteratively and incrementally. Since the project is large and deliverables are vague, it might not be possible to make the project scope clearer and remove ambiguity before starting implementation. In that case, the predictive approach would be more suitable than agile. Needless to say that the agile coach's role does not involve clarifying the scope of work, it rather entails helping the project team embrace an agile mindset. Defining all of the iterations needed for completing the project refers to predictive planning. Likewise, project baselines are only specified in predictive projects.

Question 14 = D

Explanation: A team charter is a document that is developed in a group setting to clarify team direction while also establishing boundaries. It is created at the team's forming phase in order to encourage understanding and buy-in. A team charter aligns the team with ground rules, team values, meeting guidelines, working agreements, as well as other group norms (PMBOK 7th edition, page 192).

Question 15 = B

Explanation: Lessons learned meetings are collaborative retrospective sessions for discussing, documenting, and soliciting feedback about the project's successes and missteps. These meetings are a must for the project team to learn from previous mistakes and improve future processes and projects. Lessons learned meetings should be held whenever needed, to review the way a project has been progressing, note important learnings, and set new ways for amelioration. Team building activities aim to increase collaboration among team members. Kick-off meetings are meant for communicating the objectives of the project and ensuring the stakeholders' commitment to the project. Risk review meetings are used to verify the status of existing risks and identify new ones (PMBOK 7th edition, page 180). However, capturing lessons learned from current or closed risks commonly happens in the lessons learned meetings.

Question 16 = A

Explanation: Focus groups bring together stakeholders and subject matter experts to interactively discuss and learn about their expectations and attitudes towards a proposed service, product, or result (PMBOK 7th edition, page 15).

Question 17 = C

Explanation: In any business, customers or sponsors have to be the highest priority when delivering a product. It's not enough to deliver a functioning product; the product must work for the customer or the sponsor's needs.

Question 18 = D

Explanation: Variance analysis is a technique used at the end of a project or phase in order to identify any deviation in deliverables or difference between actual and planned behaviors. This method is used to determine the cause and magnitude of the difference between baseline and actual performance, as well as retain control over the project (PMBOK 7th edition, page 177).

Question 19 = D

Explanation: In projectized organizations, all activities are managed through projects. Upon completion of the project, the project manager releases the team members to move on to the next project. Quality inspections are performed before getting the client's approval. Unlike functional organizations, projectized organizations have no functional managers, and if they do, their role and authority are quite limited. Checking whether all project tasks are completed should be also carried out before delivering the final product to the client since it's part of the quality audit.

Question 20 = B

Explanation: When you want to resolve a conflict, a face-to-face meeting is always the best first step. Hence, the project manager should meet with the manager of the supplier's team to discuss the issue and try to find a solution. Other communication methods, such as sending an email or having a phone call, are less effective than an in-person meeting. If direct negotiation fails, then the project manager should proceed with Alternative Dispute Resolution (ADR), such as mediation or arbitration.

Question 21 = C

Explanation: A release of 110 story points takes 6 sprints to be completed by a team that has 20 story points' velocity. Even though dividing 110 by 20 equals 5.5 sprints, the number of iterations should be an integer since the predetermined timebox of a sprint should not be changed. In Scrum, it's possible to calculate the estimated number of sprints as long as the velocity of the team and the estimation of the workload are known. But, you need to keep in mind that this is an estimation rather than a commitment since changes could happen along the way.

Question 22 = B

Explanation: The project manager should notify the sponsor of any identified risks that may impact the business value of the project. Business value measurements are used to ensure that the project deliverables remain consistent with the business case and benefits realization plans. Business value can be financial or non-financial (PMBOK 7th edition, page 102). A make-or-buy analysis is considered a tool for measuring financial business value. The sponsor can determine whether to continue the investment or not if the payback period turns out to be more than 3 years after updating the make-or-buy analysis. The project manager should not update the make or buy analysis report without consulting or referring to the sponsor first. If the project is following a predictive approach, it can show assuring SPI and CPI, especially at the beginning of its execution. However, since the developer's rate was underestimated, the project will get off-track in terms of cost later on. If the sponsor agrees to carry on the project and increase its budget according to the new findings, then a change request should be issued. However, when following an adaptive approach, no change requests, SPI, or CPI are used. In this case, the project manager should inform the sponsor or the product owner about their findings and discuss whether it's still possible to achieve the project goals or not.

Question 23 = B, C, D

Explanation: Backlog refinement (formerly referred to as backlog grooming) occurs when the product owner along with some, or all of the team members checks the backlog to make sure it contains the proper items, that these items are prioritized, and that the ones at the top are ready to be delivered (PMBOK 7th edition, page 235). This activity is carried out regularly and can be either an officially scheduled meeting or an ongoing activity. The process of developing the initial list of product requirements represents backlog elaboration or creation.

Question 24 = A

Explanation: The decision tree analysis is used to support the identification and selection of the best course of action among several alternatives. Each of these alternative paths can have associated costs and risks, including both threats and opportunities. The decision tree reveals the expected monetary value of each branch, allowing the determination and selection of the optimal path (PMBOK 7th edition, page 175).

Question 25 = D

Explanation: Agile project managers generally follow the servant leadership style, which consists in leading through serving the team. Servant leadership focuses on capturing and addressing the needs of team members in order to achieve good team performance (PMBOK 7th edition, page 17). Participative leadership, aka democratic leadership, involves soliciting team members' input while decision-making rests on the participative leader. Autocratic leadership is when the leader makes all decisions on their own. Transformational leadership is when the leader motivates their team and enhances their productivity through high visibility and communication.

Question 26 = B

Explanation: Since it is a local custom, the project manager should accept the gift and inform management. Project managers should refrain from accepting or offering gifts, payments, or any form of compensation for personal gain unless it is in accordance with the laws or customs of the country where the project is being executed. Rejecting or returning gifts may be considered inappropriate and rude in some cultures. The best thing to do in such a situation is to accept the gift and then inform their management.

Question 27 = C

Explanation: In a predictive approach, Lag is when an activity is complete and there is a delay before the subsequent activity starts (PMBOK 7th edition, page 59). For example, in order to paint a room, you need to first apply the primer coating, then you have to let it dry for two days before applying the final coat of paint. These two days of waiting for the primer coat to dry are referred to as Lag Time.

Question 28 = A

Explanation: Since the question states that stakeholders were already identified and that the project didn't start yet, stakeholder analysis is the right answer. Stakeholder analysis refers to the classification of all project stakeholders in order to ensure efficient engagement later on. Stakeholder engagement takes place in the execution process group and it involves: communicating and collaborating with stakeholders to meet their expectations, addressing issues, and fostering appropriate stakeholder involvement. Stakeholder monitoring implies assessing stakeholders' satisfaction and whether their engagement plan is effective or it needs to be updated (PMBOK 7th edition, pages 11-12-14).

Question 29 = A, B, C

Explanation: When issues occur, the right course of action implies informing the client of what happened, suggesting potential solutions for the issue, and then submitting a change request. This is aligned with the philosophy stating "don't bring me problems, bring me solutions" (PMBOK 7th edition, page 28). Later on, when the issue is fixed, a lessons-learned meeting should be conducted to avoid similar problems in the future. Holding the information and not updating the customer on what's going on with the project can have a bad impact, both on the project and its manager's transparency.

Question 30 = B

Explanation: A project manager's power is considerably low in a weak matrix organization. In fact, they are rather considered a coordinator or an expediter. It's up to the functional manager to assign resources in such organizations. Therefore, the only solution to obtain the needed resources in this situation is by negotiating your requirements with the functional manager.

Question 31 = B

Explanation: The user story written by the product owner is not specific and cannot be tested. Even if it's written in a user story format it's vague and unclear. The product owner must specify what new functionality they were looking to develop. It's possible to include financial values in a user story as long as they contribute to making it more clear and more understandable. A goal can be time-bound, i.e., a SMART goal, but a user story is not bounded by time.

Question 32 = A, D

Explanation: Scrum uses empirical data to measure work progress, therefore the project manager should let the product owner know that, based on current performance, the release plan is not feasible. The product manager can update the release plan or study with the project manager the possibility of adding more resources to the team. The capacity of the team is around 36 story points, and it wouldn't be possible to motivate the team to consistently reach 50 points on each sprint. Besides, a sprint has a timeboxed duration which should not be extended for any reason.

Question 33 = B

Explanation: The project manager can help their team get self-organized by mentoring them on how to make their own decisions. This will empower them to pick their own tasks without waiting for assignments or asking for permission or direction from the project manager every time. Taking a vacation is a passive approach to dealing with the problem and it won't solve it since the team will get back to relying on the project manager as soon as they come back. Ensuring that the team includes different functional expertise will help the team be cross-functional rather than self-organizing. Supporting the team by removing encountered impediments is part of the agile project manager's duties and won't help make the team self-organizing.

Question 34 = B

Explanation: The results are precise because all measurements are close to 4.45mm (+ or - 5mm). Precision entails delivering end-products with similar dimensions, which may or may not be close to the required dimensions. Precise measurements are not necessarily close to the target value; they're just close to one another. Accuracy, however, implies creating products with close dimensions to requirements.

Question 35 = C

Explanation: The larger the Net Present Value (NPV), the more profitable the project will be for the organization. A positive NPV indicates that the investment is worthwhile.

Question 36 = A, B, D

Explanation: All options, with the exception of project management certification, represent interpersonal skills. According to the PMBOK, interpersonal skills include communication styles assessment which implies identifying the appropriate communication format, method, and content for each situation, political awareness which helps the project manager plan communication according to the project environment, and cultural awareness to understand the differences between groups, individuals, and organizations, hence adapting the project's communication strategy to these differences (PMBOK Guide 6th Edition, page 375).

Question 37 = C

Explanation: The CPI (Cost Performance Index) is a measure of the conformance of the actual work completed (EV, Earned Value) with the incurred Actual Cost (AC): CPI = EV / AC = $2,000 / $1,000 = 2 which means that the project is under budget. The Schedule Performance Index measures the conformance of actual progress to the planned progress (SPI = EV / PV). Since the PV is unknown, we can't find out if the project is behind or ahead of schedule.

Question 38 = C

Explanation: SWOT stands for Strengths, Weaknesses, Opportunities, and Threats. It's a tool that project managers use to assess the opportunities and threats they might face, as well as their projects' strengths and weaknesses (PMBOK 7th edition, page 177). Assessing the project's business model or conducting a benefit/cost analysis could be part of developing the business case, but both methods have a different purpose from the SWOT technique. The PDCA cycle is a quality management technique to control and continuously improve processes and products.

Question 39 = B

Explanation: The product owner is responsible for placing the clearest and most valuable items at the top of the product backlog. Consequently, less valuable items will be dragged to the bottom. Product backlog items should not be organized chronologically or according to their difficulty level.

Question 40 = C

Explanation: Since the project is complex, frequent communication is required. Therefore, the best option is to schedule regular meetings once or twice a week, with the possibility of attending standup meetings to get daily updates. Monthly meetings, even if they're face-to-face, are not efficient for complex projects. Giving access to the project management software is considered pull communication since the sponsor has to seek information themself. Pull communication might not be sufficient for high-power demanding stakeholders.

Question 41 = D

Explanation: Agile teams should not be involved in portfolio planning since it falls under the sponsor or product owner's responsibilities. Portfolio planning or portfolio management involves determining which projects are a good fit for the organization, in which sequencing they're going to be managed, and for how long. Agile teams are only concerned with these three levels of work planning: Release planning, iteration planning, and daily planning. Release planning handles user stories that will be developed in the new release of the product. The next level is iteration planning which is conducted at the start of each iteration. Finally, daily planning or daily stand-up meetings are used to coordinate work and synchronize daily efforts.

Question 42 = B

Explanation: Providing training on technologies related to the work item will help the team fully understand how it should be executed. This strategy aims to mitigate the risk by reducing conflict between team members. The other options involve either avoiding the risk by outsourcing the work item, accepting it by letting the team figure out a solution on their own, or escalating the risk to the functional manager.

Question 43 = A, B, D

Explanation: Poor resource planning, limited documentation, and fragmented output are three key downsides of the agile approach. Since Agile is built on the fact that teams don't know what their final result will look like earlier in the project, it's difficult to anticipate project costs, time, and resources at the start, and this difficulty becomes more pronounced as projects become larger and more complex. Moreover, in Agile, documentation occurs during the project, and it is often done "just in time", rather than at the beginning of the project. As a consequence, documentation becomes less informative. Additionally, while incremental delivery can help launch goods faster, it's often regarded as one of the Agile approach's major disadvantages: when teams work on each component at different time periods, the end result often becomes fragmented instead of being one coherent deliverable. On the other hand, Agile teams are self-organizing which is proven to contribute to a higher velocity, increased quality, and less need for team management.

Question 44 = B

Explanation: Based on the direction of the hierarchies within the organization, there are two basic types of communication: Horizontal and Vertical. In horizontal communication, the project manager communicates with their peers or people on their organizational and hierarchical level. However, in vertical communication, communication flows from a lower level to a higher level and vice versa, as described in the question. "Parallel" and "triangular" communication are made-up terms.

Question 45 = B

Explanation: Trying to convince upper management requires the use of interpersonal skills, which are often needed when acquiring resources. The project manager may lack planning skills since she didn't identify the resource requirement from the beginning, but this situation does not tackle this aspect or the need to respond to the risk associated with adding more resources. In case the manager accepts her request, the project manager may not need to go through the hiring process if resources are already available within the organization.

Question 46 = B

Explanation: Agile teams don't focus on how to predict the project work; instead, they try to focus on high-priority tasks, getting early feedback, and adopting the servant leadership approach.

Question 47 = A

Explanation: Management reserve is used to deal with unidentified risks, aka "unknown-unknowns". Management reserve is part of the project budget, but it's not part of the cost baseline. It is not an estimated reserve either; it is rather defined according to the organization's processes and policies. It can represent 5% of the total project cost, for example. As the name indicates, this reserve is controlled by management and not by the project manager. Therefore, any usage of this reserve should be pre-approved by management (PMBOK 7th edition, page 242).

Question 48 = C

Explanation: The described scenario involves an example of pull communication. PMBOK defined three types of communication: interactive, push, and pull. Proactive communication is a made-up term. Pull communication is a communication type where access to the information is provided, however, the receiver must proactively seek out and retrieve this information. When the communication is solely for informative purposes, pull communication should be used. It will have little to no impact on the project if the recipients do not read it. According to the PMBOK guide: "Pull communication is used for large complex information sets, or for large audiences, and requires the recipients to access the content at their own discretion subject to security procedures. These methods include web portals, intranet sites, e-learning, lessons learned databases, or knowledge repositories." (PMBOK Guide, 6th Edition, page 374).

Question 49 = A, C

Explanation: Helping someone do a task properly and focusing on people's well-being are the main behavioral aspects and characteristics of servant leaders. However, rewarding high-performing employees is considered transactional leadership, whereas inspiring people fall under the charismatic leadership style.

Question 50 = B

Explanation: The stakeholder register document contains all relevant information concerning the project stakeholders including their influence, interest, involvement, and potential impact on the project's success. External vendors are considered project stakeholders and therefore they should take part in the stakeholder register. The project manager should refer to this document whenever they need any information concerning both internal and external stakeholders.

Question 51 = A

Explanation: First, the development team should collaborate with the product owner in order to remove some work items from the sprint backlog. The sprint backlog is a living artifact that should be updated whenever something new is learned or discovered. Afterward, in the sprint retrospective, the team should discuss how they can improve their estimations. The agile team should be proactive and should not wait for the sprint review in order to inform the product owner that they couldn't complete the affected work. Reprioritizing the product backlog items won't help solve this problem. This activity is often undertaken during the refinement sessions with the purpose of making user stories ready for the following iterations.

Question 52 = A, B

Explanation: The project team should perform a qualitative risk analysis. If they find that the risk must be prioritized, a detailed risk response should be then developed. All identified risks should be added to the risk register. During the project execution, all occurring issues are noted in the issue log. Monitoring the risk development is undertaken during the execution phase too, not the planning phase.

Question 53 = B

Explanation: The planned work is included in the lowest level of the WBS components, known as work packages. Detailed information on work packages, such as descriptions, owners, prerequisites, successors, due dates, etc. is included in the Work Breakdown Structure Dictionary (PMBOK 7th edition, page 253).

Question 54 = A

Explanation: Projects get authorized by someone external to the project such as the sponsor, PMO, or portfolio steering committee (PMBOK 6th edition, page 77). Unless the Project sponsor is part of Senior Management, the project charter should be signed by someone with the authority to assign project resources and name the project manager, i.e., the project sponsor. The project manager or stakeholders may under no circumstances sign the charter to authorize the project.

Question 55 = B

Explanation: Tacit knowledge, aka implicit knowledge, is the type of knowledge that can't be transferred to another person by means of writing or verbalizing. Examples of tacit knowledge include insights, beliefs, experience, and know-how. The opposite of tacit knowledge is explicit, formal, or codified knowledge (PMBOK 7th edition, page 70).

Question 56 = C

Explanation: A corporate knowledge base is part of the Organizational Process Assets. Enterprise Environment Factors (EEFs), however, include procedures, policies, and legislation that has an impact on how the project manager manages a project (PMBOK 7th edition, page 239). Examples of EEFs include Organizational culture, Market standards and conditions, Codes of conduct, Quality standards, Work authorization systems, Risk databases, etc. (PMBOK 6th edition, pages 38-39).

Question 57 = A

Explanation: The Code of Ethics and Professional Conduct states that project managers should cooperate with any investigation concerning ethics violations, which includes providing any information related to the violation.

Question 58 = D

Explanation: Rolling wave is a project planning method that consists of a gradual elaboration of details to the Work Breakdown Structure (WBS) over time. Near-term deliverables are decomposed into individual components (work packages) that are broken down to the greatest degree of detail. Long-term deliverables, on the other hand, are identified more broadly. In this way, rolling wave planning allows work to progress on current and near-term deliverables while the planning for potential work packages continues. The Rolling wave method is used to address uncertainty rather than prioritizing, organizing, or sequencing activities (PMBOK 7th edition, page 249).

Question 59 = A

Explanation: When the project sponsor decides to terminate the project for any reason, the project manager should follow their instructions and terminate the project. In this case, they should immediately start the "close project" process. This scenario doesn't describe any disputes between the project manager and the sponsor concerning contracts' terms, consequently claims administration is not the right answer.

Question 60 = C, D

Explanation: Most probably, stakeholders are losing interest in the project because their input or feedback is being disregarded, or they are not seeing any tangible progress. The project manager has to engage stakeholders by taking their feedback into consideration to show them that their ideas are valued. The project manager should also demonstrate working increments as early in the project lifecycle as possible. This is considered one of the advantages of the agile approach that stakeholders expect and appreciate. Sending reminders before each meeting or allowing for anonymous feedback does not yield more engagement as both options don't address the root cause of the problem.

Question 61 = B

Explanation: Fixed price contracts are used for projects with clear requirements where a price is fixed in return for the seller's services and/or products. Time and Material (T&M) contracts set a quote for an hourly rate plus the cost of materials instead of quoting a fixed price for the entire project. Cost Reimbursable contracts, on the other hand, reimburse the contractor for the actual costs they incur to provide their services and/or product, plus an additional fee. A Cost Plus Incentive contract, for instance, is a cost-reimbursable contract that incentivizes the contractor to bring their best performance by completing the project under budget or before deadlines.

Question 62 = B

Explanation: As a problem-solving technique, the Five whys is used to explore the underlying cause of a defect or an issue. By asking successive "Why?" questions, the team digs deep to figure out what went wrong and thus be able to determine how to properly address the problem and how to avoid similar issues in the future.

Question 63

Explanation:

A. Construction work requires a building permit from the City council: EEF

B. Workers who don't obey safety rules will be penalized: OPA

C. Only authorized personnel are allowed on site: OPA

D. Workers have expertise in infrastructure construction: EEF

Question 64 = C

Explanation: A War room, aka situation room, or command center, is a space where people come together to address issues through enhanced workflows and clear communication. Since it's a physical space, a war room can't be one of the advantages of acquiring a remote team. On the other hand, having access to more skilled resources, reducing commute time, and having less travel and relocation expenses are all among the many advantages of employing remote resources.

Question 65 = B

Explanation: When joining a new organization, it is very important that the project manager grasps the organization's culture. Although talking to executive managers and project managers may help in this matter, understanding the culture, i.e., how the organization operates, its policies, and its appetite for risk, among other things should be the project manager's first priority when joining a new organization.

Question 66 = B, C

Explanation: Bidder conference, aka contractor conference or vendor conference, is arranged to ensure that sellers have a common understanding of the project procurement requirements (PMBOK 7th edition, page 70). During the conference, the project manager and the stakeholders will discuss their procurement needs and answer any questions the sellers might have. In a bidder conference, the project manager does not shortlist prospective sellers or award the contract.

Question 67 = A

Explanation: A portfolio is a grouping of projects and programs. A portfolio's purpose is to establish centralized management and oversight for a number of projects and/or programs. It also helps establish standardized governance across the organization. By creating and managing a portfolio, you're ensuring that the organization is choosing the right projects that align with its values, strategies, and goals (PMBOK 7th edition, page 244).

Question 68 = A

Explanation: The knowledge acquired from the process of carrying out a project is referred to as "lessons learned."

This covers both the positive and negative aspects. The aim is to replicate good practices and avoid repeating errors. By failing to examine or go over past lessons learned, the project manager risks making the same errors as in previous projects. Therefore, the earlier the lessons are identified and embedded into a project, the more value they will provide. So ideally, a project manager should conduct reviews on an ongoing basis to allow for continuous improvement. Such a review will capture in-depth inputs from the project team, sponsors, stakeholders, etc. Capturing and going over lessons learned on a regular basis helps keep the project on track. In the long term, it will also help organizations continuously develop and enhance the way they conduct projects.

Question 69 = B

Explanation: The critical path comprises tasks that must be completed as scheduled in order for the project to be finished on time. If a task is delayed, it may cause a delay in the project's completion date. Some tasks on the critical path may not be critical themselves, but they need to be accomplished on time in order for the critical task(s) to be completed (Fundamentals of Technology Project Management by Colleen Garton, Erika McCulloch, pages 238-239). The critical path method is used in projects following a predictive life cycle where change requests could have a direct impact on the project.

Question 70 = A

Explanation: The project manager should talk to the senior project manager privately to get to know the reason behind their behavior. Besides, the project manager should be clear about not tolerating any kind of discriminating behavior towards the new team member and the potential consequences and disciplinary procedures the senior team member will face in case their behavior persists. The project manager should talk directly to the concerned party with no need for escalating the issue to the functional manager at this stage. Such behavior should not be ignored, even when it seems to have no tangible impact on work progress. On the other hand, it's not appropriate nor professional to scold a team member in a meeting and in the presence of their colleagues, regardless of their behavior.

Question 71 = C

Explanation: The project manager should evaluate the impact of the delay before making any decision. A delayed activity doesn't necessarily result in the whole project delay. For instance, if the activity is not on the critical path and it has a lag of more than three days, then the delay won't probably have any impact on the project. Therefore, there is no need for negotiating the delay or looking for a new vendor to get the order delivered on time.

Question 72 = D

Explanation: The Issue Log is a project document where all information concerning faced issues is recorded and monitored (PMBOK 7th edition, page 336). Even though the described scenario involves lessons learned (never to deal with the unreliable vendor in the future), the question only inquires about where to record the issue.

Question 73 = B
Explanation: Lag Time is when a delay is purposely made between activities. Lead time, on the other hand, is the time saved by starting an activity before its predecessor is completed. Crashing and fast-tracking are two schedule compression techniques.

Question 74 = A
Explanation: Risk transfer involves transmitting future risks from one party to another. A common example of risk transfer is purchasing insurance where the risk of a person or an organization is transferred to the insurance company. Asking the sponsor to deal with the risk is an escalation rather than a risk transfer. Other risk response strategies include avoiding, mitigating, or accepting the risk (PMBOK 7th edition, page 123).

Question 75 = A
Explanation: At the end of each iteration, the project manager and the project team should demonstrate a potentially shippable product increment to the concerned

stakeholders along with the Product Owner to get their feedback. This occurs during an Iteration Review Meeting. The product owner and stakeholders use this meeting to evaluate the product and release backlog priorities (PMBOK 7th edition, page 180).

Question 76 = A, B, C
Explanation: Destructive testing loss is an example of the cost of conformance, the rest fall under the cost of non-conformance. Cost of Non-Conformance includes the expenses arising due to non-conformance to quality requirements.

Cost of Non-Conformance can be divided into two categories:

1. Internal Failure Costs are incurred when defects are detected internally (i.e. not yet presented to the customers) which include defect repair and rework.

2. External Failure Costs are incurred when defects are discovered after the deliverables have been shipped to customers (this is the worst type of quality cost) These include warranty work, liabilities, and loss of business goodwill.

Reference: PMBOK 7th edition, page 89.

Question 77 = B
Explanation: Project management involves applying a set of processes, skills, knowledge, experience, and methods, to attain a number of predefined project objectives and

requirements according to predetermined acceptance criteria (PMBOK 7th edition, page 17).

Question 78 = A, D

Explanation: Prototyping is a technique used to collect early feedback on the requirements for further refinement and clarification, along with clarifying ambiguities (PMBOK 7th edition, page 246). The development of a prototype can either increase the project cost and duration or reduce them depending on its results.

Question 79 = D

Explanation: Voting is used to reach a consensus decision by selecting the option which gets more votes from the team members. This technique is simple, intuitive, and both time and cost-efficient. Since both options have a negligible cost, no risk, and a short implementation period, it wouldn't be adequate to allow the discussion to take more time, nor to set up a formal meeting or escalate the matter to the project sponsor.

Question 80 = B

Explanation: Asking another team member to help mentor the new member and guide them through getting their task completed and overcoming the challenging aspects of their assignment is the right course of action. Since the member is new and they might lack certain skills or experience dealing with certain types of tasks, they will get the chance to learn and overcome any impediments by collaborating with more experienced team members. Assigning someone else to get the task done will only have a bad impact on their self-esteem and motivation and make them miss out on a learning opportunity. Similarly, expressing their disappointment at the new member's performance will do more harm than actually resolving the issue. Checking the team ground rules is irrelevant to this situation.

Question 81 = C

Explanation: Regardless of the fact that the change was requested by a member of the CCB, the project manager should submit a change request according to the procedures defined in the change control system. This system describes how modifications to project deliverables should be undertaken (PMBOK 7th edition, page 332). The change request is not submitted yet to the CCB, so it should not be recorded in the change log. After submitting it, the change log should be updated to track the status of the change. The project manager should not implement the change without getting the CCB's formal approval. Being convinced of the change's value or having the consent of one member of the CCB is not sufficient to move forward with the implementation.

Question 82 = B

Explanation: The project manager is mitigating the risk of resource attrition. This type of risk response aims to diminish the probability and/or impact of a threat (PMBOK 7th edition, page 123).

Question 83 = B, C

Explanation: This is an example of finish-to-finish mandatory dependency. Two tasks may in fact run concurrently in the case of a finish-to-finish dependency. However, the second task can be entirely completed only after the first task is 100% done. Mandatory dependencies are those that are legally or contractually required or inherent in the nature of the work (PMBOK 7th edition, page 60).

Question 84 = B

Explanation: The 5% limit represents stakeholders' tolerance, which is an enterprise environmental factor. These factors determine how a project manager leads a project. So, it is important for the project manager to have a good understanding of the EEFs that could affect their project.

Question 85 = A

Explanation: Check sheets, aka tally sheets, are used to gather facts in order to facilitate the collection of more data concerning a potential quality issue (PMBOK 7th edition, page 175). A checklist, on the other hand, is used to verify whether a set of required steps has been performed or not.

Question 86 = C

Explanation: Passive risk acceptance is an appropriate approach when it is best to handle the risk when it does occur. No proactive action is needed for passive acceptance other than periodically reviewing the threat to ensure that it does not change significantly (PMBOK 7th edition, page 123).

Question 87 = D

Explanation: The functional manager is the one in charge of managing resources under a weak matrix. This matrix form has a huge resemblance to a traditional workplace hierarchy. A functional manager is a project's main decision-maker as they supervise all of its aspects. Although the project manager also serves as a point of authority, they primarily report back to the functional manager.

Question 88 = B

Explanation: When dealing with complex issues, such as updating a plan or dealing with legal matters, it would be best to document such discussions and decisions using a formal written format. According to the PMBOK 6th edition (Page 499): "The buyer, usually through its authorized procurement administrator, provides the seller with formal written notice that the contract has been completed. Requirements for formal procurement closure are usually defined in the terms and conditions of the contract".

Question 89 = C

Explanation: In order to effectively lead the project, the project manager should be fully aware of the project's purpose, priorities, and deliverables. After examining the goals and deliverables included in the project charter, the project manager should create a transition plan to help the project team cope with the unexpected change, check the project logs and reports, reassess what has been accomplished so far, and maintain the team's commitment to the project goals and priorities.

Question 90 = D

Explanation: First, the project manager should understand the impact of the team member's departure on the project. It might have a big impact therefore the leaving member needs to be promptly replaced with an experienced member. Or, their departure might have a limited impact and the project can proceed without their contribution. Based on the evaluation findings, a decision should be taken on whether to get a replacement or reassign the workload. The project's resource breakdown structure should be updated later on to reflect the new changes.

Question 91 = D

Explanation: Since the project manager has received an approved change request, they should ensure its appropriate implementation. Since the change request specifically entails the replacement of the defective component, the project manager shouldn't repair it instead.

Question 92 = C
Explanation: This chart is a burndown chart that shows that there is work left at the end of the sprint (PMBOK 7th edition, page 108). In fact, 3 story points are left to be completed in order to finalize all the planned work for the exhibited 7-day sprint.

Question 93 = B
Explanation: The schedule performance index (SPI) is a measure of the conformance of actual progress (earned value) to the planned progress: SPI = EV / PV (PMBOK 7th edition, page 249). A value of 1.0 indicates that the project performance is on target. When CPI or SPI is greater than 1.0, it indicates better-than-planned project performance, while a CPI or SPI that is less than 1.0 indicates poorer-than-planned project performance.
EV = 10% x $100,000 = $10,000, PV = (1 Month / 10 Months) x $100, 000 = $10,000 then SPI = EV / PV = 1.

Question 94 = A
Explanation: Planning poker is a card-based technique that is mostly used for estimating project activities. It is a consensus-based estimating technique (PMBOK 7th edition, page 58). It can be used with story points, ideal days, or any other estimation unit. The estimation is done using

poker cards. Team members discuss the feature, asking the product owner any questions they might have. Then, privately, each team member picks out one card that presents their estimate. All cards should be then revealed at once. If all team members select the same value, it's set as the final estimate. Otherwise, a discussion of the different opinions and estimates will take place again before re-estimating the feature or task again.

Question 95 = C

Explanation: External dependency is the relationship between project activities and external activities that are not related to the project. Even though it's beyond the project team's control, such a dependency should be reflected in the project schedule. On the other hand, discretionary dependencies, also referred to as soft logic, preferred logic, or preferential logic, are not mandatory (PMBOK 7th edition, page 60).

Question 96 = B

Explanation: Voting is a technique for collective decision-making which can be used to generate and prioritize project requirements. Unanimity, plurality, and majority are examples of voting techniques. A majority decision requires being supported by more than 50% of the group members.

Question 97 = C

Explanation: To ensure the successful delivery of the project, the project manager should first define success criteria with the sponsor. Agreeing upon the project's success criteria will reduce the possibilities of its failure and reinforce its success odds. When determining the project success criteria, you should avoid using unclear and general terms and focus on being precise and clear. It's recommended to be specific by saying, for instance: "the product should be completed by November 30th" instead of saying "the product should be completed as soon as possible".

Question 98 = D

Explanation: With an adaptive approach, the project's cost and schedule are fixed, while the scope can be adjusted to stay within the cost constraint. Consequently, the project manager needs to prioritize the most important features when planning each release until they exhaust the whole budget. All other options imply using the predictive approach, which won't work for this project since its scope is unpredictable.

Question 99 = B

Explanation: A timebox is a fixed period of time in which work has to be completed. The timebox duration could be a few hours, days, or weeks depending on the work complexity or size (PMBOK 7th edition, page 181).

Question 100 = D

Explanation: As a facilitator, the project manager must ensure that all attendees take part in the meeting by encouraging them to share their ideas and opinions and engaging them in the discussed topics. It's among their responsibilities as a facilitator to ensure that everyone takes part in the decision-making, problem-solving, brainstorming, etc. activities that take place during meetings. Promoting participation and maintaining the ideas and discussions flow during such events is an indication of efficient facilitation. Changing meetings from face-to-face to virtual or limiting their duration does not guarantee more engagement or participation. Moreover, limiting the intervention of talkative participants will only result in more inactive attendees.

Question 101 = C

Explanation: Because projects are temporary endeavors, most of the acquired knowledge is lost once the project is completed. The project manager should be attentive to knowledge documentation and transfer to allow the organization to gain and retain the knowledge and experience obtained through running projects (PMBOK 7th edition, page 78). Once this activity is completed, a celebration could take place and resources can be released. On the other hand, the change log should be updated to monitor the change requests' status.

Question 102 = B

Explanation: The project manager should involve the key stakeholder from the very beginning of the project to help reduce and uncover risks, as well as increase her "buy-in." While implementing an agile approach may benefit the project, it does not address the issue of stakeholder management. If the question were "what's the appropriate approach for the project?", then adopting an agile approach would be the right answer taking into consideration the frequently changing requirements.

Question 103 = D

Explanation: The bottom-up method can be used as an estimation technique for the project's overall cost by estimating the approximate value of smaller components and using the total sum of these values to find the overall cost. This type of estimation is used to create the project schedule or budget. The project work is typically subdivided into smaller parts and each component is given a duration and cost estimate. The individual duration estimates are aggregated to determine the schedule, while the individual cost estimates are aggregated to determine the budget.

Question 104 = B

Explanation: Corrective actions are reactive as they're performed to fix issues that have occurred to bring the project back into alignment with the baselines. Preventive actions, on the other hand, are proactive as they're taken to ensure that the project doesn't deviate from the plan. Both corrective and preventive actions can be part of the executing process group as well as the monitoring process group.

Question 105 = A

Explanation: Knowledge can be either explicit or tacit knowledge. Explicit knowledge can be expressed and captured using pictures, words, and numbers. Tacit knowledge, such as experiences and beliefs, is more difficult to express or capture (PMBOK 7th edition, pages 77-78).

Question 106 = B

Explanation: A secondary risk is a risk caused by a response to a primary risk; the secondary risk would not exist if the risk response was not taken.

Question 107 = C

Explanation: Tailoring involves the selection of the appropriate processes, related inputs and outputs, techniques, and life cycle phases in order to manage a project (PMBOK 7th edition, page 6). Project management is the application of a set of knowledge, skills, tools, and techniques to project activities to meet the project requirements. Program management, on the other hand, is the application of knowledge, skills, tools, and techniques to meet the program requirements.

Question 108 = A, D

Explanation: This project's concrete benefits for pharmaceutical companies involve increasing revenue and reducing charges, by getting tax deductions for instance, which are considered tangible benefits. Reputation and brand recognition, on the other hand, are intangible benefits.

Question 109 = D

Explanation: When the project is closed or terminated for any reason, the project manager should start the close process. Procurement closure is part of the "Close project" process. The situation in the question requires project termination, so the correct answer implies executing the process that addresses the situation, i.e. the Close Project process. Plus, there is no indication in the question that the project has procurements.

Question 110 = C

Explanation: Short daily meetings are referred to as daily standup meetings which represent a framework for sharing what each member has accomplished, what they will be doing next, and what blockers they're facing. This type of meeting helps build a connection between team members, improves communication, and as a result reduces rework. Co-location can resolve this issue too. However, team members are dispersed in different countries, making it difficult to assemble them in one location. Offering team members training about cultural differences could only help them overcome cultural barriers, but it can't help them sync their work to avoid rework. Written, asynchronous communication such as emails does not promote bonding or building connections in comparison to verbal synchronous channels such as virtual meetings.

Question 111 = C

Explanation: Appraisal costs, also known as inspection costs, are part of the Cost of Conformance as they represent the costs of identifying defective products before they are delivered to clients. This comprises testing, inspecting, auditing, evaluating, and measuring the deliverables, products, or services the project is producing. Appraisal costs are set up to implement a series of activities to determine work results' degree of conformance to quality requirements. Meaning the project appraisal cost involves inspection costs which are $5,000. Training falls under prevention activities. Rework and scrap costs, on the other hand, are part of the Internal Failure Costs, whereas Warranty charges fall under External Failure Costs.

Question 112 = C

Explanation: Waterfall is a predictive methodology that was deemed too rigid to handle the changing requirements brought on by new technology or a demanding client. Even though there are numerous Agile and Lean frameworks, the

Agile Practice Guide only addresses Scrum, Kanban Method, Scrumban, eXtreme Programming (XP), Crystal Methods, Dynamic Systems Development Method (DSDM), Feature-Driven Development (FDD), and Agile Unified Process.

Question 113 = A

Explanation: A resource calendar is a calendar for planning, managing, and monitoring resources, including both employees and equipment. It gives project managers an overview of how resources are being utilized, which resources are available, and when. On the other hand, the Responsibility Assignment Matrix (RAM) describes the involvement of different parties and their roles in completing tasks or deliverables in a project. It's used to clarify roles and responsibilities within a team, project, or process. RACI is an acronym for Responsible Accountable Consult and Inform and it's used to assign roles and responsibilities for each task in a given process. An organigram, also called an organizational chart, organogram, or organizational breakdown structure (OBS), is a diagram that depicts the organization's structure and the relationships and ranks of its different positions.

Question 114 = A

Explanation: The iterative method is the heart of the Agile development process. Each iteration generates a piece of the product until the final product is fully completed and delivered.

A typical iteration process flow involves:

- Analysis: to define the iteration requirements based on the product backlog, sprint backlog, and feedback from customers and stakeholders.
- Development: includes design and implementation based on the defined requirements.
- Testing: involves Quality Assurance testing.
- Delivery: integrating the working iteration into production,
- Feedback: receiving customer and stakeholder feedback to define the requirements of the next iteration.

Question 115 = B

Explanation: Grade refers to a category or rank given to entities having the same functional use but different technical characteristics. A product can be of a high-grade (high-end) or low-grade (low-end). A low-grade product is perfectly acceptable, as long as it fulfills requirements. On the other hand, a low-quality product is always a problem and is never acceptable. Every produced item must have high quality regardless of its grade; no one wants a low-quality product. Example: You buy a basic model (low-grade) cell phone with no advanced features, but it works well. Thus, we're talking about a high-quality product. Although it is low-grade, it keeps you satisfied (PMBOK 7th edition, page 241).

Question 116 = B

Explanation: In such situations, the project manager should not pay and should instead follow the chain of command and solicit their support in providing security to the project team. This situation is considered bribery or at least palm greasing. Nevertheless, the project manager should act proactively and take all security measures.

Question 117 = C

Explanation: A murder board is a committee of experts that critically evaluates project proposals. Project representatives have to answer the critical questions raised by the committee members in what looks like an oral exam. The murder board scrutinizes the project by looking for and pointing out reasons why the project should not be considered. The main responsibility of the murder board is to critically and aggressively review the proposed project, while it's the proposer's mission to reply to each and every query of the board members to prove the worth of the project.

Question 118 = D

Explanation: The head of investments is clearly unwilling to help, which means that they are a resistant stakeholder. They can't be considered unaware because they are just pretending to be unaware in order to avoid collaborating with or supporting the project manager. The head of customer relations, on the other hand, is responsive whenever the project manager meets them in the hallway, so they can't be considered resistant. However, this does not mean they are supportive since they never reply to the project manager's emails. Hence, the head of customer relations is showing neutral behavior; they are too busy to collaborate and don't seem to care a lot about helping the project manager. In addition to being unaware, resistant, and neutral, the stakeholder engagement assessment matrix also includes supportive and leading classifications.

Question 119 = B

Explanation: During the sprint retrospective meeting, all the good and bad aspects of the sprint are discussed. The retrospective meeting is considered a meeting for improvements, as it is mainly held to find the proper ways and means of identifying potential pitfalls and past errors, and to seek out new ways to avoid those mistakes. This meeting isn't held at the end of the project's last sprint; it recurrently takes place after the Sprint Review and before the following Sprint Planning. A backlog refinement meeting is used to refine product backlog items. The sprint planning meeting is used to define and evaluate the work of the next sprint.

Question 120 = A, C

Explanation: The project manager should provide their team with relevant training in order to enable them to adopt the new agile practices with more confidence. They should also gradually introduce certain iterative or incremental techniques to make the transition smoother. This will improve the team learning process and accelerate delivering value to sponsors. Many teams can't make a full immediate switch to the agile approach. It is preferable and even recommended to make a gradual transition by combining adaptive and predictive practices, which is known as a hybrid approach (Agile Practice Guide, page 30).

Question 121 = D

Explanation: In the project closing phase, the project team including the project manager, should implement the associated processes to formally complete or close a project (PMBOK 7th edition, page 171). It's important that the closing process is done formally by following the defined procedures to avoid any future liabilities. Procedures are either established by the organization for internal projects or mutually determined by the customer and the provider in the project contract or master-level agreement (PMBOK 7th edition, page 76). Completing project work by accomplishing all tasks in the scope, fixing defects, or updating documents, is not sufficient to avoid penalties. These activities, among others, should be formally approved by the customer first.

Question 122 = D

Explanation: According to the Agile Practice Guide, servant leadership implies leading your team by focusing on understanding and addressing their needs to yield the best performance possible (PMBOK 7th edition, page 17).

Question 123 = C

Explanation: A resource breakdown structure is a hierarchical list of team and physical resources related by category and resource type that is used for project planning, management, and control (PMBOK 7th edition, page 187). Each descending level corresponds to a more detailed description of the resource. A resource calendar, on the other hand, is a calendar for planning, managing, and monitoring resources. Organizational Breakdown Structure (OBS), also known as Organization Chart, is used for representing the project organization. RACI is an acronym for Responsible Accountable Consult and Inform and it's used to assign the roles and responsibilities of the individuals involved in a project or a process.

Question 124 = B

Explanation: Negotiating is the most important skill for project managers to have when working with extremely limited budgets and resource allocations.

Question 125 = C

Explanation: The Sprint Review is a product-centered meeting, during which the agile team demonstrates the functionalities they have completed during the sprint, seeking the Product Owner's feedback and approval (PMBOK 7th edition, page 179).

Question 126 = C
Explanation: The Bottom-up estimation technique is used when project requirements are decomposed into small, feasible work elements which are then aggregated to estimate the cost of the entire project. The Bottom-up technique can be used to provide a precise estimate of both the project cost and duration.

Question 127 = A, C
Explanation: The condition of supporting one thousand visitors per hour is considered a requirement and an acceptance criterion for the project. A requirement is defined as "a condition or capability that is necessary to be present in a product, service, or result to satisfy a business need." (PMBOK Guide 7th edition, page 82). Acceptance criteria are conditions required to be met before deliverables are accepted. This condition cannot be considered a deliverable or scope on its own. Deliverables refer to quantifiable products or services that must be delivered by the end of the project, i.e., the flight booking website. The project scope, on the other hand, represents the overall

amount of work required to achieve the project's main objectives.

Question 128 = A

Explanation: The team charter is the right document to include rules and guidelines on how the team members should interact with each other (Agile Practice Guide, page 20 & PMBOK 7th edition, page 192). By adding the rule to the team charter, team members will have to adhere to it and refrain from discussing politics at work. The Resource management plan, on the other hand, covers staffing acquisition, timetable, training needs, recognition and rewards, release criteria, compliance, and safety. The project charter includes a brief description of the project and its requirements. The resource charter is a made-up term.

Question 129 = C

Explanation: Management reserve involves the dedicated budget or time reserve for handling unidentified risks or unknown unknowns (unknown = unidentified, unknowns = risks). This type of reserve is not a calculated budget and does not take part in the cost baseline. Therefore, anytime an unknown risk occurs, the project manager will need permission to use this reserve. On the other hand, a contingency reserve is used for identified risks with predetermined risk response strategies, aka known-unknowns (known = identified, Unknowns = risks) (PMBOK 7th edition, page 127).

Question 130 = B

Explanation: The project life cycle that can be adopted for developing a mobile app project is: Wireframing, prototyping, designing, developing, testing, and deploying. A project life cycle comprises the different development phases that a project goes through from its start to its completion. Depending on different factors, a project lifecycle often includes Feasibility, Design, Build, Test, Deploy, and Close phases (PMBOK 7, pages 33 - 42). Initiation, planning, executing, monitoring and controlling, and closing are process groups rather than project lifecycle phases. Forming, storming, norming, performing, and adjourning are team development phases according to Tuckman's theory.

Question 131

Explanation: The project total amount is composed of the management reserve and the project budget, which in turn is composed of the cost baseline and contingency reserve (PMBOK 7th edition, page 63). Therefore, A = Management reserve, B = Project budget, C = Contingency reserve, and D = Cost baseline.

Question 132 = A

Explanation: A change-driven approach is also referred to as an adaptive, Agile, flexible, or change-focused approach. This development approach is characterized by the ability to react and adapt to high levels of change as well as the constant involvement and participation of different parties. On the other hand, a waterfall or predictive approach is sequential and rigid. Hybrid is a combination of predictive and adaptive approaches.

Question 133 = B

Explanation: The amount of budget deficit or surplus at a given point in time expressed as the difference between Earned Value(EV) and the Actual Cost (AC), is known as Cost Variance (PMBOK 7th edition, page 238).

Question 134 = D

Explanation: The project manager must demonstrate transparency regarding their decision-making processes. Communication and reasoning about decisions concerning the project should be well-documented and accessible to everyone on the team. Transparency in project communication allows team members to see all aspects and decisions of a project that may affect or be of interest to them (PMBOK 7th edition, page 20).

Question 135 = C

Explanation: Accuracy describes how close a measurement is to an accepted value. Precision describes the statistical variability of produced measurement (it can be far off the accepted value) (PMBOK 7th edition, page 55).

Question 136 = C

Explanation: The duration of a milestone is zero because it denotes a significant achievement, point, or event in a project, such as the completion of a particular deliverable for instance (PMBOK 6th edition, page 186).

Question 137 = A

Explanation: The project manager and their team used the mind mapping technique. In a mind map, several options get discussed and then visually organized. The illustrated diagram is not a decision tree because it doesn't display or help the team choose the best decision among the different alternatives for gathering end-user feedback. On the other hand, this diagram is not an affinity diagram either, as it does not classify a large number of ideas into groups. Options A, B, and C are all data representation methods, which makes option D "Data representation" too generic to be considered the correct answer.

Question 138 = C

Explanation: Apart from the development team, nobody should decide the stories' order in the sprint backlog. Instead, team members should define their own task-level work and then self-organize in any manner they feel best to achieve the sprint goal (Essential Scrum by Rubin, Kenneth

S, page 23). The agile coach should keep in mind that the "sprint backlog" is different from the "product backlog". A sprint backlog is the set of items that the cross-functional team selects from the product backlog to work on during the upcoming sprint. The sprint backlog represents the primary output of sprint planning.

Question 139 = B

Explanation: Planning activities in an adaptive approach entails progressively elaborating the work scope based on the stakeholders' continuous feedback. The project is split into iterations, and at the end of each iteration, the customer reviews the accomplished work on the product. Then, the customer's feedback is used to define the detailed scope of the next iteration. Defining all iterations' work before the start of the project depicts an iterative development approach while implementing activities described in the statement of work depicts a predictive development approach.

Question 140 = A

Explanation: Organizational Process Assets (OPAs) include organizational processes and procedures, and corporate knowledge base. To know more about the past project's performance, the project manager could check the concerned project files such as its scope, schedule, cost, and quality baselines, in addition to its administrative documentation, stakeholder register, issue log, and any other relevant documents. These form the corporate knowledge base, and only checking the issue log might not be sufficient to figure out why the previous project went through a lot of difficulties. Additionally, you cannot find the details of the past project's performance in the Enterprise Environmental Factors (EEF) since the latter represent the conditions that have an influence on the project but are beyond the team's control. Even though the new project is agile and the previous one is predictive, it's recommended to take advantage of its documented lessons learned. Eventually, the challenges that the previous project went through might not be even linked to its adopted approach.

Question 141 = D

Explanation: The project manager should keep both the contract and the project open until the seller performs the inspection. Closing a project entails conducting several processes and steps including closing out all contracts. Closing a contract in return requires verifying that the seller has delivered their work as predetermined in the contract.

Question 142 = A

Explanation: The project manager should refer to the project charter to find the 'high-level description' of the project. The project charter is a formal document that describes the project in its entirety, including its objectives, work processes, and stakeholders. This project planning document can be used throughout the whole project lifecycle (PMBOK 7th edition, page 184). User stories and epics only represent the detailed requirements, not the entire high-level description of the project scope. The Work Breakdown Structure (WBS) also outlines the detailed requirements of projects that follow a predictive approach.

Question 143 = D
Explanation: Project constraints are limiting factors for your project that can impact delivery, quality, and overall project success. An imposed delivery date or a predefined budget are considered project constraints (PMBOK 7th edition, page 72).

Question 144 = A, C, D
Explanation: Lessons learned sessions are performed for the purpose of learning from mistakes in order to avoid repeating them in the future. They also serve as an opportunity to identify and establish best practices and build trust with stakeholders and team members. Lessons learned meetings should not be used to hold others accountable for mistakes made during the project (PMBOK 7th edition, page 180).

Question 145 = B
Explanation: S-Curves visualize the evolution of a project cost over a period of time. The name is derived from the

S-shape that data usually form, with low costs at the project's start and end, and increasingly elevated costs mid-project.

Question 146 = C, D
Explanation: Facilitation means assisting others in dealing with a process, reaching an agreement, or finding a solution without personally or directly getting involved in the process, discussion, etc. For the facilitator to maintain an impartial position, they should approach the discussion as an unbiased voice.

Question 147 = C
Explanation: Money spent during or after the project execution due to poor quality is referred to as the Cost of Non-Conformance. Internal and External Failure Costs fall under Non-Conformance Costs. Internal failure costs are failure costs that are associated with defects found by the project team before the product gets released, such as Rework or Scrap costs. External Failure Costs, on the other hand, are failure costs associated with defects found by the customer, meaning costs incurred after the product is delivered to the customer, such as costs of Warranty work, Liabilities, Lost business, etc.

Question 148 = B
Explanation: Flexibility and adaptability are the core principles of Agile. All other skills can be developed over

time when the Agile team gets to learn from its own experiences.

Question 149 = D

Explanation: In a functional organization, the project manager doesn't manage the budget. Thus, they should escalate the need for additional funds to the functional manager. If the functional manager validates their assessment, they will need to escalate their request to the project sponsor to approve allocating additional financial resources. If the project manager was working in a projectized or strong matrix organization, they wouldn't need to raise their request for more funds to the functional manager. The product owner's role is limited to the scrum framework, which is an adaptive approach. If that was the case, the project manager would need to report similar issues to the product owner, who will escalate the matter to the project sponsor. A program manager, as the name suggests, only handles programs, which is not the case in this scenario.

Question 150 = D

Explanation: Since the sponsor requested the cost estimate on short notice, in an early stage of the project with little to no information available to conduct cost estimations, the most practical method for the project manager to respond to the sponsor's query is to rely on similar past projects' data to estimate their current project cost. This entails using analogous estimating to calculate the project costs based on the known costs of a similarly completed project. Along with historical data, this technique relies on the project manager's expert judgment. The only person responsible for creating the product backlog items is the product owner, so the first option can't be realized by the project manager. Developing the Work Breakdown Structure (WBS) is not an option too, since it requires the project team's involvement in the process and it's improbable for it to be done in one day.

Full Mock Exam 1 - Result Sheet

Assign "1" point to each question answered correctly, and then count your points to get your final score.

1. ___	20. ___	39. ___	58. ___	77. ___	96. ___	115. ___	134. ___
2. ___	21. ___	40. ___	59. ___	78. ___	97. ___	116. ___	135. ___
3. ___	22. ___	41. ___	60. ___	79. ___	98. ___	117. ___	136. ___
4. ___	23. ___	42. ___	61. ___	80. ___	99. ___	118. ___	137. ___
5. ___	24. ___	43. ___	62. ___	81. ___	100. ___	119. ___	138. ___
6. ___	25. ___	44. ___	63. ___	82. ___	101. ___	120. ___	139. ___
7. ___	26. ___	45. ___	64. ___	83. ___	102. ___	121. ___	140. ___
8. ___	27. ___	46. ___	65. ___	84. ___	103. ___	122. ___	141. ___
9. ___	28. ___	47. ___	66. ___	85. ___	104. ___	123. ___	142. ___
10. ___	29. ___	48. ___	67. ___	86. ___	105. ___	124. ___	143. ___
11. ___	30. ___	49. ___	68. ___	87. ___	106. ___	125. ___	144. ___
12. ___	31. ___	50. ___	69. ___	88. ___	107. ___	126. ___	145. ___
13. ___	32. ___	51. ___	70. ___	89. ___	108. ___	127. ___	146. ___
14. ___	33. ___	52. ___	71. ___	90. ___	109. ___	128. ___	147. ___
15. ___	34. ___	53. ___	72. ___	91. ___	110. ___	129. ___	148. ___
16. ___	35. ___	54. ___	73. ___	92. ___	111. ___	130. ___	149. ___
17. ___	36. ___	55. ___	74. ___	93. ___	112. ___	131. ___	150. ___
18. ___	37. ___	56. ___	75. ___	94. ___	113. ___	132. ___	
19. ___	38. ___	57. ___	76. ___	95. ___	114. ___	133. ___	

Total:

N° of Correct Answers	% of Correct Answers
.... / 150	....

Full Mock Exam 2 - Questions

Question 1

A product owner for a high-quality clothing project joins the project team and other prominent stakeholders for a meeting to review a demonstration of a produced deliverable. Since the project adopts an iteration-based Agile approach, this type of meeting is held _____.

- **A.** At the beginning of every iteration
- **B.** At the end of every iteration
- **C.** At the end of the project
- **D.** At the start of the project

Question 2

An Agile project manager is leading an IT project using the Scrum framework. While the team implements user stories during the sprint, what should the product owner do?

- **A.** Add more tasks for the team so they can deliver more value
- **B.** Let the team do their work and respond to any questions they might have
- **C.** Protect the team from interruptions and facilitate discussions
- **D.** Monitor the sprint progress and extend its duration if the team cannot complete the assigned work on time

Question 3

A project manager must assign a complex task to one of the team members. The project manager had to choose between two members who were both equally capable of fulfilling the task. But, the project manager had a closer relationship with one of them than the other. What should the project manager do?

A. Disclose the situation to the appropriate stakeholders and solicit a joint decision

B. Choose the one that they have a closer relationship with since that type of trust can benefit the project

C. Choose the member they're not close to in order to avoid misunderstandings

D. Ask a third team member to take the decision in order to avoid a conflict of interest

Question 4

A project is 50% complete. During its planning phase, the project manager divided the project into 4 consecutive phases. Now that phase 2 is completed, they're moving on to phase 3. Based on the following table, how much is this project's Earned Value (EV)?

Phases	Planned Value (PV)	Actual Cost (AC)
Phase 1	$2,000	$3,000
Phase 2	$2,000	$3,000
Phase 3	$3,000	
Phase 4	$3,000	

A. $4,000

B. $5,000

C. $6,000

D. $10,000

Question 5

A senior manager has informed the project manager that they will be in charge of leading a Fintech (Financial Technology) project. The project manager is excited about this project since it's big and innovative, and it will present a great accomplishment in their career. However, after a few weeks, the project manager starts to feel worried because every time they inquire about the project's start date, the senior manager says that they are waiting for an official document to be issued in order to start working on the project. Which document is the senior manager referring to?

A. Project charter

B. Project management plan

C. Scope statement

D. Enterprise resource planning

Question 6

Match the following Scrum events with the corresponding activities in the table below:

Sprint planning - Sprint execution - Sprint retrospective - Sprint review

Activities	Scrum Event
A. Inspects progress towards the sprint goal	----------------------
B. Presents the project's performance to the stakeholders	----------------------
C. Discusses the improvements that can be applied in the upcoming sprints	----------------------
D. Provides estimates of the required effort to complete user stories	----------------------

Question 7

A project manager is in charge of a software development project that follows an Agile approach. During the project execution, they receive a request from the customer to alter a requirement. What should the project manager do?

A. Block the change request

B. Welcome the change request

C. Avoid the change request

D. Take the change request to the Change Control Board (CCB)

Question 8

A project manager is managing a project that consists of developing new software for a client. The project manager is collaborating with the client, business analysts, developers, and marketing team, on the project's outcomes and requirements. Who gets to decide the project's scope?

A. The business analysts

B. The client

C. The project manager

D. All of the above

Question 9

After getting assigned to manage a distressed project, a project manager reviews the schedule to find out that the previous project manager did not take into consideration procurement delays. Which of the following options represents this scenario?

A. Critical path activity

B. Schedule variances

C. Assumption

D. Constraint

Question 10

A project manager is leading an Agile project where the team works in a continuous flow rather than using iterations. This approach proved to be less prescriptive and disruptive to the team. Which Agile framework is the project manager using?

A. Scrum

B. Adaptive

C. Incremental

D. Kanban

Question 11

Facing a quality issue, a project manager decides to use the _____, a basic quality management tool that uses the 80/20 Rule to identify top-priority defects.

A. Fishbone Diagram

B. Pareto Chart

C. PERT Chart

D. Flowchart

Question 12

At the end of the iteration, a graphic designer for a dairy brand informs the project manager that she wasn't able to finish one of her assigned tasks due to an issue with her laptop. In order to prevent such a situation from occurring in the future, the project manager should:

A. Discuss the issue during the demonstration session

B. Address the issue during the following iteration planning meeting

C. Handle the issue during the next daily standup meeting

D. Discuss the issue during the retrospective meeting

Question 13

A project manager is in charge of a project that has an anticipated duration of 12 months and a $120,000 Budget at Completion (BAC). Equal amounts of project work should be completed each month. However, in the fourth month of the project, only 20% of the work was completed. The project manager spent $20,000 to finish the project. How much is the project's earned value?

    A. $40,000

    B. $24,000

    C. $20,000

    D. Cannot be determined due to insufficient data

Question 14

To keep up with everything going on with their project, a project manager relies on emails as a medium to communicate with the project team and stakeholders. To write efficient emails, the project manager uses all of the following techniques, except:

    A. Brief, right-to-the-point expressions

    B. Consideration of the reader's needs

    C. Words and ideas fluency

    D. Tone variation

Question 15

During a prospect meeting, the client insisted that the new website they want to develop must meet some crucial conditions: it must be SEO (Search Engine Optimization) friendly, with a score of 80% or above, and all of its pages must be responsive on all devices and screen sizes. The client is setting the website's _____.

A. Definition of Done

B. Quality Assurance

C. Functional Requirements

D. Fit for Use

Question 16

During a training session, and in order to clearly explain what a project can be, a project management coach gave their trainees the following example:

A. Saving an endangered species of rhinos from extinction

B. A weekly clean-up of the local park

C. A shoe factory that produces 1000 pairs monthly

D. Preparing pasta for your family every Monday

Question 17

Organizations often attempt to deliver projects with limited budgets and incomprehensive requirements. An Agile approach can be adopted to address such complexities. However, without proper communication, this approach won't achieve its goals. Under this context, how should a project manager communicate?

A. Informally

B. Formally

C. Frequently

D. Daily

Question 18

A project manager is leading a project that was supposed to last 6 months. The project is currently in its second year. Which of the following statements best describes the situation?

A. The project scope was not clearly defined

B. The project should have been divided into subprojects

C. The project team didn't protect the scope from changes

D. The project should have been halted after 6 months

Question 19

A project manager is assigned to a construction project of a new housing complex that is expected to take fourteen months. During the last planning session, the project team finished decomposing the project deliverables. Which of the following documents was produced during this meeting?

A. Work Breakdown Structure (WBS)

B. Organizational Breakdown Structure (OBS)

C. Resource breakdown structure

D. Requirements documentation

Question 20

A project manager is leading a rebranding project using a predictive approach for the planning phase and an Agile approach for work execution. The project manager receives an email from a key stakeholder requesting an estimation of the project completion date. In order to estimate the completion date, the project manager takes into consideration the team's average velocity, which is 20 story points, and the fact that the project still has 205 remaining user story points to complete. How many iterations will it take to finish the project work?

A. 10 iterations

B. 11 iterations

C. 12 iterations

D. Cannot be determined

Question 21

A product owner started the day with a sprint planning meeting to discuss and define the goal and backlog of the upcoming sprint. Which of the following options is correct regarding the sprint planning meeting?

A. A discussion between the product owner, the scrum master, and the cross-functional team

B. A discussion between the cross-functional team members only

C. A discussion between the product owner and the scrum master

D. A discussion between the scrum master and the cross-functional team members

Question 22

Velocity generally enables project managers to make predictions that are accurate, but not totally precise, concerning project planning. The term "Velocity" in scrum refers to?

    A. A team's sprint-by-sprint progress rate

    B. Project execution speed

    C. Team members' average capacity

    D. All of the above

Question 23

Which of the following actions depicts smoothing?

    A. The project manager postpones taking a decision about the issue to a later time

    B. The project manager makes a decision with the assistance of the most experienced team member

    C. The project manager takes into consideration the opinions of both parties when making a decision

    D. The project manager downplays the issue between conflicting parties

Question 24

A project manager is managing a project using the predictive approach. A Change Control Board (CCB) is formed, in which the project sponsor is a member, to review all change requests. One month after the project launch, the CCB received three change requests; the first was by the sponsor, the second was by a low-power stakeholder, and the third one was issued by a senior team member. Which of these individuals is not allowed to submit a change request?

- **A.** The sponsor since they are a member of the CCB
- **B.** The stakeholder since they have low power
- **C.** The senior team member since they are part of the project team
- **D.** All of the above are allowed to submit a change request

Question 25

After completing all requirements, the project manager sits with the product manager to go over each item of the deliverable acceptance criteria. The product manager found that among thirty deliverables, two did not meet requirements, so they asked the project manager to make the necessary changes before signing off the final delivery document. Which process are they both currently performing?

- **A.** Control quality
- **B.** Control scope
- **C.** Validate scope
- **D.** Close project

Question 26

A project manager is pitching an innovative project idea in an entrepreneurial event to get the needed investment. To ensure that they engage both the audience and the jury during the pitch, the project manager should:

   A. Point her finger

   B. Make eye contact

   C. Wave her hands

   D. Stand up straight

Question 27

One month into project execution, the project manager notices that the sponsor is always late for their weekly meetings. However, the project manager chooses not to address the sponsor's behavior. Instead, they document the frequent tardiness in the meetings' notes. Which conflict resolution technique is the project manager using?

   A. Problem-solving

   B. Smoothing

   C. Information recording

   D. Withdrawal

Question 28

A(n) _____ helps stakeholders check out the status of material shortage, technical difficulties, scheduling conflicts, etc., and how they're being monitored and treated.

   A. Feedback log

   B. Issue Log

C. Sprint backlog

D. Change log

Question 29

A project manager collaborates with the project team to create the Work Breakdown Structure (WBS) for their project. What purpose does this document serve? (Select two)

A. Help the project team define the project scope

B. Help the project team visualize the project work

C. Help the project team organize the project scope

D. Help the project team identify the project requirements

Question 30

A project manager uses the scrum framework to manage a graphic design project. Which of the following events will not be used by the project team?

A. Sprint planning

B. Weekly scrum

C. Sprint review

D. Sprint retrospective

Question 31

The burnup and burndown charts are tools used by Scrum teams to get an overview of a sprint's work development. Both charts are primarily used for:

A. Identifying technical issues

B. Tracking project progress

C. Project retrospective

D. Sprint planning

Question 32

"Impediments" are usually evoked during daily standups, and in some cases, they are thoroughly discussed during the sprint retrospective. "Impediments" refer to:

A. Issues that hinder the Agile team's project completion

B. Change requests

C. External risks

D. Problems caused by the product owner

Question 33

When performing earned value measurements, a project manager finds out that the Cost Performance Index (CPI) of their project is 0.91. What does this indicate?

A. The project is behind schedule

B. The project is ahead of schedule

C. 91% of project work is finished

D. The project is over budget

Question 34

Working in a risk-averse organization, the project manager suggested using the agile approach for a new project that has a high level of uncertainty. How should risk management be conducted in this case? (Select two)

A. The project manager will own the risk management

B. Both the project manager and the project team conduct risk analysis, determine risk responses, and update the Risk Register

C. The project team analyzes and addresses risks in all planning meetings, with a focus on qualitative rather than quantitative analysis

D. Risks are monitored through the use of information radiators, stand-up meetings, iteration reviews, and retrospectives

Question 35

Which factor should be considered during Sprint Planning?

A. Number of stories in the product backlog

B. Number of stories completed in the last sprint

C. Team velocity

D. Team size

Question 36

What is the Scrum Master's role during the daily stand-up?

A. Congratulate the team when they do a good job

B. Listen to the team for any faced impediments

C. Ask each team member what they accomplished since the last daily standup

D. This meeting is for team members only, the Scrum Master should not attend

Question 37

Now that the project is nearly finished, a key stakeholder asked the project manager whether they were nervous about the project deliverables approval process, to which the latter replied that they were confident that the customer will be satisfied with the result. What can ensure the satisfaction of the project's customer?

A. The project's low running costs

B. How good the project manager's relationship is with the project's end-users and stakeholders

C. The efficiency of the warranty service

D. Delivering value and conforming to project requirements

Question 38

A Project manager ensures that the project team documents all assumptions. The team records assumptions on an ongoing basis and then validates these assumptions. Which of the following helps the team validate a project assumption?

A. Organizational policies

B. Historical data

C. Constraints

D. Team members recollection

Question 39

The project cost is lower than the project manager had anticipated. The project manager must spend all of the first phase's allocated budget, otherwise, the budget of the second phase will be reduced. To use up the assigned budget for the first phase, the project manager decides to purchase better instruments to offer the client higher-quality deliverables. This scenario depicts:

    A. Integrated change control

    B. Effective cost management

    C. Gold plating

    D. Budget compliance

Question 40

A project manager is using the Agile approach to manage a software development project. During a meeting with the team, the project manager presents the _____ to showcase how much work still needs to be done during the current iteration.

    A. Schedule

    B. Burnup chart

    C. Milestone chart

    D. Burndown chart

Question 41

Depending on who is using them, bids, tenders, and quotes can take on different meanings. But, initially, all of these terms can be used interchangeably with:

    A. Proposals

    B. Make-or-buy decisions

    C. Buyer responses

    D. Pre-bid conferences

Question 42

8 tasks of an Agile project release have the following story points: 3, 2, 5, 5, 8, 1, 3, 5. Given that the team's velocity is 10, how many iterations will they need to complete all of the 8 tasks?

    A. 3

    B. 4

    C. 5

    D. 7

Question 43

In order to monitor and track the progress of project performance, the organization's management uses earned value measurements. Which of the following values is an indication that a project has issues?

    A. A CPI of 0.89

    B. An SPI of 0.99

    C. A CPI of 1.01

    D. A BAC of $100,000

Question 44

A sales representative of a luxurious hotel chain asked a local carpenter, who owns a small workshop specialized in designing and manufacturing outdoor furniture, to produce a single unit of a new concept of egg chairs as quickly and inexpensively as possible. What is this product called?

    A. Pre-production version

B. Product increment

C. Minimum viable product

D. Sample

Question 45

A project manager is assigned to an amusement park project. The project comprises two phases: the first phase involves importing attractions like games and rides, and the second entails setting up and installing everything. What should the project manager do after completing the first phase?

A. Validate scope

B. Identify risks

C. Identify stakeholders

D. Define activities

Question 46

A project manager is working in an organization that provides products on the cloud. After a 6-month study, the organization's R&D department approved a project which will permit internet navigators to create cartoon videos using stock images, gifs, and short video clips. There will be only a \$20/Month pricing plan. What type of project does this describe?

A. Large project

B. Internal project

C. Agile project

D. Traditional project

Question 47

A project manager presented a stadium construction project that they believe will benefit the community tremendously. Despite the mayor's agreement to carry out the project, the project manager encountered strong resistance from various stakeholders since the beginning. What should the project manager do to resolve this problem?

A. Create a Responsibility Assignment Matrix (RAM) to indicate which stakeholder is responsible for what aspects of the project and who needs to be consulted or informed

B. Create an organizational diagram to assign each stakeholder to the appropriate project role, allowing or disallowing certain lines of communication

C. Schedule a meeting with the concerned stakeholders to thoroughly explain the project, discuss and establish ground rules, ensure their involvement, and identify any personal or organizational issues that might surface later on

D. Avoid contacting these stakeholders at the start of the project and instead create a "faits accomplis" to pressure them to support the project due to a lack of alternatives

Question 48

A project manager is assigned to lead a new project that has a predetermined budget of $170,000. Which of the following options does this situation illustrate?

A. Assumption

B. Expert judgment

C. Constraint

D. Functional structure

Question 49

A project manager consults a group of the organization's subject matter experts on some points concerning his project. In order to ensure objectivity, the experts provided their input anonymously in order to prevent the influence of one opinion on the others. Which method is the project manager using?

A. Expert Judgment

B. Delphi Technique

C. Brainstorming

D. Focus groups

Question 50

The traditional format of a daily stand-up meeting consists of gathering in a circle near a task board where each member takes their turn to answer a number of questions. Which of the following statements best describes the daily stand-up in agile?

A. It is a meeting during which the upcoming work schedule is discussed

B. It is a meeting during which the team is asked about what they did on the previous day and their plan for the current day along with any problems they might have faced during the execution of their tasks

C. It is a daily brainstorming session

D. It is a daily lessons-learned session

Question 51

During an iteration review meeting, the product owner rejected one of the features demonstrated by the development team. What will happen next to the rejected user story?

A. It will be automatically moved to the next sprint backlog

B. It will be deleted from the product backlog and from the project

C. It will be updated to address the reasons why it was rejected

D. It will be moved back to the product backlog for reprioritization

Question 52

A project manager was assigned to organize a national chess tournament. The tournament project has been planned and approved for execution. Three months separate the project manager from the big event, during which they will follow the scrum approach with 2-week long sprints. Before starting any work, they hold a meeting with the sponsor, project team, stakeholders, and key contractors. What kind of meeting did the project manager hold?

A. Sprint planning meeting

B. Kick-off meeting

C. Status meeting

D. Scoping meeting

Question 53

A project manager has been collaborating with the project sponsor to address a number of quality and risk-related issues. Which of the following statements concerning the role of the sponsor is true?

A. The sponsor takes part in managing the project with the project manager

B. The sponsor provides the project manager with the needed resources for completing the project

C. In a functional environment, the sponsor gives the project manager the freedom to make all decisions related to the project

D. The sponsor can get involved in assigning team members to particular project tasks

Question 54

During the sprint retrospective meeting, team members complained that they were always wasting time going back and forth with the product owner to schedule the backlog refinement meeting. The project manager suggested creating a recurring event to fix the issue. When should this event take place?

- **A.** Right after the sprint retrospective
- **B.** Right before the sprint planning
- **C.** Right after the sprint planning
- **D.** At any time during the sprint

Question 55

A project manager is leading a business transformation project. As part of the project scope, a survey with 10 experts has to be conducted. During project execution, the project sponsor asked to raise the number of experts to 20, explaining that 10 experts might not provide enough input and insight. The sponsor also requested making this adjustment without issuing a change request. What should the project manager do?

- **A.** Accommodate the change
- **B.** Refuse to make the change
- **C.** Negotiate the number to reach a consensus
- **D.** Inform the sponsor that they need to follow the change management process

Question 56

A project is behind schedule since the functional manager reassigned three team members to other projects. After negotiating with the functional manager, the project manager agreed to a temporary solution that would enable them to get one team member back for the time being, with a follow-up discussion after two weeks to re-address the issue. What conflict resolution technique did the project manager employ in this situation?

A. Compromise

B. Force

C. Collaborate

D. Smooth

Question 57

A project manager attended a meeting to finalize a procurement that was still in the negotiation stage. However, they noticed that discussions tend to drift to various irrelevant topics, with attendees occasionally going back to the meeting's main topic. What is this meeting missing? (Select two)

A. Minutes

B. An agenda

C. An objective

D. A facilitator

Question 58

After getting assigned to manage a distressed project, a project manager reviews the schedule to find out that the previous project manager did not take into consideration procurement delays. Which of the following options represents this scenario?

A. Critical path activity

B. Schedule variances

C. Assumption

D. Constraint

Question 59

A project manager is assigned to lead a recycling project. During the project planning phase, the defined scope was approved by management and all stakeholders. During the execution of the project work, two key stakeholders ask the project manager to change a particular part of the scope statement. What should the project manager do?

A. Ask the stakeholders to submit a change request

B. Refuse to alter the scope since it has already been approved by all stakeholders

C. Refuse to alter the scope since it cannot be modified after being officially approved

D. Refer the stakeholders to the project sponsor

Question 60

A project manager works for Massive Fun, a company specializing in eco-friendly kids' toys. Two months into the project, they launch the second phase consisting in developing biodegradable playing dough. Hence, the project manager meets with the sponsor to check if any potential players were left out in the first phase and to discuss these new stakeholders' influence. The activity that the project manager is carrying out with the sponsor can be identified as:

A. Planning stakeholder engagement

B. Identifying stakeholders

C. Planning resource management

D. Identifying risks

Question 61

In order to assess the project performance, a project manager calculates both its CPI and SPI. Knowing that it has a high CPI and a low SPI, what is the project status?

A. Behind schedule & under budget

B. Ahead of schedule & under budget

C. Behind schedule & over budget

D. Ahead of schedule & over budget

Question 62

In order to explain to the client the meaning of a story point in the agile methodology, a project manager states that a story point can be defined as:

A. The equivalence of WBS in the predictive approach

B. An estimate of project duration

C. An estimate of the required efforts to complete a particular task

D. A score that is given to measure the clarity of a particular task

Question 63

A project manager is in charge of the construction project of a shopping center. Project work entails involving multiple subcontractors to perform paving, road connection, and parking lot lighting activities. During the project execution, the paving contractor informs the project manager that the district has increased the cost of linking the parking lot to the city drive. Which of the following communication methods should the subcontractor use to convey this information?

A. A cost variance report

B. A formal presentation

C. A memo sent to management

D. A memo sent to the project manager

Question 64

A project manager asked a team member to prepare a presentation for an important prospect. After checking it, the project manager found the presentation comprehensive and engaging, but the outline was missing. The outline of the presentation is a list of:

A. Major headings or topics to be covered in the presentation

B. References and bibliography at the end of the presentation

C. The presentation requirements and purpose

D. External sources used in the presentation

Question 65

A project manager of a distressed project had been replaced by a new one. While the new project manager was examining the network diagram, they found five critical paths and two near-critical paths. What does this indicate about the project?

A. The project is at a high-risk

B. The project requires more financial or human resources

C. The project will be completed on time and within budget

D. The project should be terminated

Question 66

The project sponsor attended the sprint review meeting and appreciated the demonstration. Then, they requested a new feature to improve product competitiveness. How should the project manager respond to this request?

A. Welcome the change by creating a user story and adding it to the ongoing sprint

B. Create the user story, but add it to the next sprint to protect the team from disruptions

C. Create the user story and let the product owner decide its priority

D. Not create the user story since the request should come from the product owner, not the sponsor

Question 67

Match the following communication methods with their corresponding advantages in the table below: Asynchronous, Virtual, Written, Face-to-face.

Communication Methods	Advantages
A. -----------------------	Increases flexibility and reduces pressure
B. -----------------------	Builds connections and leads to more engagement
C. -----------------------	Decreases ambiguity and ensures commitment
D. -----------------------	Saves costs and limits interruptions

Question 68

A project manager is working on a 12-month project that has a predefined tight budget and rigorous quality standards. The project must be completed with no cost overruns whatsoever, otherwise, it will be deemed a failure. During execution, and due to some technical challenges, the project completion deadline could be extended, which could induce a minor increase in the project budget. Which of the following is the most critical to this project?

A. Time control

B. Scope control

C. Quality control

D. Cost control

Question 69

A project manager is leading a project for developing an online furniture store. Developing the online store internally would cost $100,000, plus a $3,000 monthly maintenance fee. When exploring the option of developing the online store externally, the project manager received an offer from a vendor to create the store for $50,000 plus $4 per transaction to administer the e-store, knowing that the online store will potentially have an average of 1000 transactions per month during the first year. Which of the following methods can help the project manager determine and choose the best option?

A. Pareto chart

B. Control chart

C. Decision tree

D. Trend analysis

Question 70

A project manager is carrying out the initial planning activities for a gas pipeline construction project using a predictive approach. When estimating the pipeline installation activity, one team member states that they ran the same length of pipes in 14 hours on a previous similar project. Another team member claims that they can run 100 meters of gas pipes per hour. The team will need to run a total of 1000 meters of pipes. Using the analogous estimating technique, how many hours will it take the team to run the gas pipeline?

A. 10

B. 11

C. 12

D. 14

Question 71

Which of the following options falls under the project manager's responsibilities in Agile?

A. Providing the overall strategic direction

B. Controlling the project budget

C. Defining user stories and prioritizing the backlog

D. Ensuring that the team delivers the project according to the defined requirements

Question 72

A project manager is responsible for leading a hybrid project with remote team members dispersed across four continents. As a result, the team has experienced communication issues. What can the project manager do to alleviate the team's communication challenges? (Select two)

A. Set up remote pairing

B. Use an agile approach for the project

C. Colocate the team

D. Create fishbowl windows

Question 73

A stakeholder is pressuring the project team to make some changes to the final product. The project manager informs the client that the changes cannot be implemented immediately due to the organization's established processes. Which of the following documents these processes?

A. The change control board

B. The change control system

C. The organizational process assets

D. The scope management plan

Question 74

Wanting to have their own home, a couple decided to avoid getting a mortgage and build a tiny house instead. After watching some videos and reading many tutorials, they started planning for the project. However, when it came to interior design, they seemed to disagree on many details. Since they wanted to get their house ready by the end of the year, they decided to launch the construction work first and decide about the interior design details later on. What technique are they using?

A. Rolling wave

B. Fast-tracking

C. Crashing

D. Decomposition

Question 75

A project manager is in charge of holding a conference about entrepreneurship. In order to be up-to-date with the current trends and understand what participants and potential attendees might look for, the project manager asked their team to perform benchmarking, brainstorming sessions, focus groups, interviews, and questionnaires. What are these tools and techniques used for?

A. Data analysis

B. Data gathering

C. Data representation

D. Decision making

Question 76

To collect more funding, a project manager sends their project's business case to an investor who happens to be quite demanding, as they might reject a project because its goal is not SMART. What does "S" stand for?

A. Specific

B. Simple

C. Smart

D. Safe

Question 77

A project manager is leading a pharmaceutical manufacturing project that follows a predictive approach. The project management team regularly communicates with stakeholders to collect their feedback and assess their engagement. In which process group do stakeholders have the most influence over the project?

A. Initiating

B. Planning

C. Executing

D. Closing

Question 78

Which of the following Fixed Price contracts should be used for currency fluctuations?

A. Fixed Price with Currency Adjustments

B. Fixed Price with Economic Price Adjustments

C. Fixed Price Incentive Fee

D. Firm Fixed Fee

Question 79

A project manager suggested that the project team should put in extra hours to complete the project on time, which was totally refused by the organization. They think that overworking the project team can have negative direct consequences on the project, including: (Select three)

A. Reduced quality of work

B. The need for more frequent quality inspections

C. Low team morale

D. Poor team performance

Question 80

A project manager is in charge of an ergonomic chair design project. Upon the identification of some technical risks, the project manager decides it's best to create a prototype. This is an example of risk:

A. Acceptance

B. Avoidance

C. Transfer

D. Mitigation

Question 81

A project manager is in charge of a software development project. Their organization primarily uses agile methods. An intern who joined the project team once asked the project manager: "What is a User Story?" How should the project manager reply?

A. A story that refers to the ideal user for your project

B. A day in the end-user life

C. A small, granular unit of work that brings added value to the customer

D. A collection of all the requirements that the customer wants in a project

Question 82

A project manager is assigned to lead a marketing project for a political party. During a phone call with the party representative, the latter requested adding social media advertisements to the project. The project manager informed the representative that they were willing to include the service for an additional $8,000, to which the representative agreed. However, when the project manager sent the invoice including the requested service fees, the representative refused to pay the additional cost. What could have been done differently to avoid this situation?

A. The project manager should have chosen a more appropriate communication channel

B. The scope could have been cut to balance the cost of the additional service

C. The project manager should have requested a lower price for the additional service

D. Nothing could have been done differently

Question 83

A project manager got the approval to carry out a significant change that would bring added value to the project. The change has a total cost of $10,000 and will add one month to the project's duration. What should the project manager do right after getting the change approved?

A. Call for a meeting with the CCB to review the change

B. Update the time, cost, and scope baselines to reflect the change

C. Perform a change risk assessment

D. Update the change control system to reflect the change

Question 84

A project manager is approached by an organization to develop the resource planning for their new innovative project. Even though the project manager has worked with many similar organizations in the past, this time, they are skeptical about the project's business model. Should the project manager use historical information in this case?

A. No, since every project is unique, there is rarely any correlation between different projects' resource expectations

B. No, since historical information is usually not applicable for innovative and rapidly changing projects

C. Yes, since historical information can provide insight when making comparisons to resources used on previous similar projects

D. Yes, since an accurate estimation of resources cannot be performed without referring to historical information

Question 85

Match the statements concerning the tasks of a hybrid project with their right classification:

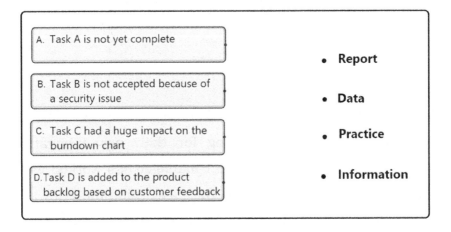

A. Task A is not yet complete

B. Task B is not accepted because of a security issue

C. Task C had a huge impact on the burndown chart

D. Task D is added to the product backlog based on customer feedback

- **Report**
- **Data**
- **Practice**
- **Information**

Question 86

In predictive projects, the scope baseline, which is usually used as a basis for future comparisons, can only be modified through formal change control procedures. What are the components of the scope baseline?

- **A.** Scope statement, WBS, and WBS dictionary
- **B.** Scope management plan and WBS
- **C.** WBS and WBS dictionary
- **D.** Project charter and Scope management plan

Question 87

A project manager is managing a project using a hybrid approach. After one week of the first iteration, the customer informs the project manager that they were dissatisfied with the deliverables. What should the project manager do next?

- **A.** Ask the customer to submit a change request so that their dissatisfaction can be addressed
- **B.** Use soft skills to convince the customer that the deliverables conform to project specifications
- **C.** Investigate the cause of dissatisfaction and verify the deliverables
- **D.** Implement adjustments and improvements in the next iteration

Question 88

To take into consideration the Triple Bottom Line, the project manager invites the sponsor to attend a meeting for defining the scope of a new project. What are the three elements of the Triple Bottom Line?

- **A.** Performance, planet, profit
- **B.** Plan, people, profit

C. Profit, people, planet

D. Profit, people, performance

Question 89

A project manager is in charge of the creation of an online catalog of the company's products. A particular team member is managing documentation. Even though this member is doing a great job, their work pace is way slower than expected, which can cause the whole project to miss its deadline. What should the project manager do first in this situation?

A. Delegate some of the concerned team member's tasks to other writers

B. Remove the concerned team member from the project

C. Find out the cause of the team member's slow work pace

D. Give the concerned team member other non-critical tasks

Question 90

A project manager working at Smart Tools, a smart kitchen appliances company, has recently completed the design phase of a product. Therefore, the project manager is currently arranging a phase review with the steering committee, which will be facilitated by the company's PMO. Phase reviews are also called:

A. Kill point

B. Endpoint

C. PMO review

D. Project review

Question 91

A project manager is leading a project using an iterative development approach. During which meeting is a potentially shippable product increment presented to the concerned stakeholders?

A. Iteration kickoff meeting

B. Iteration planning meeting

C. Iteration review meeting

D. Iteration retrospective meeting

Question 92

Due to a lack of knowledge of the involved technology, an agile team was unable to estimate the number of user stories needed in the subsequent iteration. What tool or technique can the project manager recommend to overcome such a problem?

A. Value stream

B. Progressive elaboration

C. Spike

D. Refactoring

Question 93

A subcontractor is engaged to install the electrical wiring of a construction project. A stakeholder requests a modification in the project's scope, which will result in a change in the subcontractor's workload. Which of the following documents will address how the change in the subcontractor's workload will be handled?

A. The change control system

B. The procurement management plan

C. The contract

D. The scope

Question 94

During a sprint review meeting, a team member demonstrated a new feature and pointed out that it took longer than expected due to missing technical documentation. Then, they asked a senior team member how they could avoid this in the future. What should the meeting facilitator do?

A. Let the discussion flow naturally since it's important and only intervene if the side discussion continues for too long

B. Ask the team member to reflect on how to make such improvements at another meeting

C. Interrupt the team member because the product owner is not supposed to know that documentation is missing

D. Let the discussion continue and then ask the product owner to give feedback on potential improvements

Question 95

During the project's planning, the project manager noticed that a number of stakeholders are unsupportive because they think that they will lose their jobs due to the project. What should the project manager do to overcome this problem?

A. Disregard the project's unsupportive stakeholders

B. Use the autocratic leadership style to be able to lead the project

C. Create an effective communication management plan and stakeholder engagement plan

D. Refuse to work on a project that might lead to job losses

Question 96

A team has 100 story points in the product backlog and a velocity of 30 points per iteration. Taking into consideration that the iteration is two weeks long, how many weeks does the team need to complete the backlog?

A. 4 weeks

B. 6 weeks

C. 8 weeks

D. 10 weeks

Question 97

A project manager got assigned to a new project. Prior to the project kick-off, the sponsor introduces the project manager to the organization's C-level executives and reassures them that the project is bound to be a success. Who assumes responsibility for the project's success?

A. Project sponsor

B. C-level executives

C. Project manager

D. All of the above

Question 98

What can a project manager use Source Selection criteria for?

A. Project performance assessment

B. Quality compliance inspection

C. Sellers assessment

D. Potential projects evaluation

Question 99

A project manager is leading a 3-year project that involves upgrading and improving an electric engine for industrial use. Since the majority of the project activities are hazardous, the project team will receive extensive safety training. The training will ensure the safety of workers and prevent delays caused by unsatisfactory work. The cost of the conducted safety training falls under:

A. Cost of regulations

B. Cost of Quality

C. Cost of conformance

D. Cost of nonconformance

Question 100

A project manager is in charge of a project for creating a next-generation vehicle. Before the assembly of the vehicle can be performed, the wheels have to be designed and built. Which type of dependency does this situation depict?

A. External

B. Discretionary

C. Soft Logic

D. Mandatory

Question 101

During a meeting with stakeholders, the project manager is asked about the amount of work completed by the agile team during the last sprint. What information should the project manager share with stakeholders?

A. The sprint velocity

B. The sprint backlog items

C. The average velocity

D. The forecasting velocity

Question 102

During a retrospective meeting, two team members disagree about their involvement in a recent work incident, accusing each other of dodging responsibility. To avoid such an issue in the future, the project manager decides to create a RACI matrix. RACI is an acronym for:

A. Responsible, Accountable, Confirm, Inform

B. Recommended, Accountable, Consulted, Inform

C. Responsible, Accountant, Consulted, Inform

D. Responsible, Accountable, Consulted, Inform

Question 103

Establishing a change control system is crucial for a project's success. The coordination of all changes across the whole project is part of change control. When should integrated change control be performed?

A. Throughout the whole project

B. During the project execution phase

C. During the planning phase

D. During the monitoring and controlling phase

Question 104

An organization puts too much emphasis on continuous improvement. They even have a policy that entails holding a meeting after each checkpoint in order to capture patterns of success or failure. In which of the following meetings can they discuss why things went wrong and what could be improved? (Select three)

A. Retrospective meeting

B. Lessons learned meeting

C. Status meeting

D. Post-mortem meeting

Question 105

When a dispute arose between two important stakeholders, the project manager intervened and successfully handled it, preventing further escalation. Where should the project manager take note of the arising issue?

A. Risk register

B. Issue log

C. Change log

D. Stakeholder register

Question 106

A project manager is trying to control the costs of the project they are working on. Thus, the project manager decides to calculate the _____ in order to define the value of the completed work, based on its pre-approved assigned budget.

A. Planned Value

B. Earned Value

C. Schedule Variance

D. Cost Variance

Question 107

Communication is key to the success of any project. It is particularly important when it comes to building positive stakeholder relationships. Which is the best communication method to maintain and improve relationships with stakeholders?

A. Interactive communication

B. Written communication

C. Pull communication

D. Push communication

Question 108

A project manager and their team are implementing a strategy to update the operating system of all of the company's computers. Later on, the project team discovers that not every computer supports the new version of the operating system. Which of the following statements best describes this scenario?

A. The project team made a wrong assumption

B. The project team didn't develop an appropriate project plan

C. The project team didn't establish an adequate risk response

D. The project team didn't consider the new version of the operating system as a constraint

Question 109

A project manager sets up recurring meetings in the communication management plan. Which of the following regularly held meetings will be dedicated to tracking the project's overall progress?

A. The quality review meeting

B. The status meeting

C. The kick-off meeting

D. The standup meeting

Question 110

A project manager works for a construction company, which has recently gone through major organizational changes. The organization's new manager seems to be closely monitoring when employees arrive and leave work. The project manager overhears her saying that she is concerned about the team's lack of motivation. What type of management style does the new manager exhibit?

  A. Theory X

  B. Theory Y

  C. Theory Z

  D. Theory XY

Question 111

Making the transition from a predictive to an agile scrum environment was a big move for a project manager and their team. After switching to a scrum framework, the project manager now conducts different types of meetings to ensure open communication, collaboration, and efficiency. Which of the following meetings is process-oriented?

  A. Sprint planning

  B. Sprint review

  C. Sprint demonstration

  D. Sprint retrospective

Question 112

Upon reviewing user stories, the agile coach finds out that a few ones are not following the common template format.

Which of the following formats should the agile coach instruct the development team to follow for user stories?

    A. As a <developer role>, I want to develop <feature>

    B. As a <user role>, I want to <goal>, so that <benefit>

    C. As a <stakeholder role>, I want to achieve <goal>

    D. As a <user role>, I want to <feature>

Question 113

A project manager works for a B2B marketing company. The company does not have an official archiving procedure. The project manager has recently finished a project and got the client's official approval of the final deliverables. Now that the project is in its closure phase, what should the project manager do with all associated paperwork?

    A. Nothing since the company doesn't require the archiving of performed projects

    B. Archive the project documents himself

    C. Discard it since it represents a liability

    D. Ask the client to keep the project's archive

Question 114

A sponsor submitted a change request to the Change Control Board (CCB) of which the project manager is a member. The Board counts five members, and their opinions diverged concerning whether to accept or reject the change request. What is the best course of action in order to make a decision?

    A. Try to reach a consensus

B. Call for voting and let the majority decide

C. Let the most experienced member of the board decide

D. Let the board director decide

Question 115

After defining the project's high-level requirements, the agile team along with the product owner begin writing down a list of the product features, including short descriptions of all the functionalities they're going to deliver. Next, they're going to prioritize the product backlog based on:

A. The value of the items

B. The complexity of the items

C. The size of the items

D. The risk associated with the items

Question 116

A project manager works in an IT company that strictly complies with the Agile Software Development Manifesto. All of the following are values of the Agile Manifesto, with the exception of:

A. Individuals and interactions over processes and tools

B. Working software over comprehensive documentation

C. Customer collaboration over contract negotiation

D. Following an iteration over following a plan

Question 117

A project manager is in charge of New York's new bridge construction project. They were informed by one of the subject matter experts that, next July, all of the bridge construction work will need to stop taking into consideration the past history of river flooding due to hurricane season. Thus, they agree with the expert and arrange to stop the work during that month. This decision is considered as:

A. Acceptance

B. Transfer

C. Mitigation

D. Avoidance

Question 118

A project manager has been assigned to a project that consists of constructing a bridge in their city. Missing the deadline for the project completion would make the company pay a fine for each additional day of delay. Which of the following does this example best illustrate?

A. Assumption

B. Cost constraint

C. Critical path method planning

D. Schedule constraint

Question 119

A project manager is assigned to a construction project of a new housing complex that is expected to take fourteen months. During the last planning session, the project team finished decomposing the project deliverables. Which of the following documents was produced during this meeting?

A. Work Breakdown Structure (WBS)

B. Organizational Breakdown Structure (OBS)

C. Resource breakdown structure

D. Requirements documentation

Question 120

When conducting remote resource hiring, what is the best way to quickly collect data from candidates to analyze and compare?

A. Video recordings

B. Workshops

C. Questionnaires and surveys

D. Live interviews

Question 121

A project manager is managing an urban housing construction project. They identified a risk that might affect work execution due to an equipment malfunction. Which of the following risk response strategies should the project manager use? (Select two)

A. Exploit

B. Enhance

C. Mitigate

D. Avoid

Question 122

During the project charter development phase, the project manager discovers a gap in the business case; some key regulatory requirements were missing. Non-compliance with these regulations could result in legal issues. Complying with these regulations, on the other hand, could result in drastic scope changes and budget overruns. What should the project manager do?

A. Issue a change request to implement the needed changes for meeting regulations

B. Consider these findings a risk and plan a response

C. Start implementing the project and decide later on how to address these requirements when a better solution can be established

D. Inform the project sponsor of their findings

Question 123

Now that the project is nearly finished, the project manager starts preparing for the archiving process by organizing the project records. Which of the following documents should be part of the project archives? (Select three)

A. Correspondences with the subcontractors

B. Contracts of remote team members

C. Memos

D. Drafts of the project charter

Question 124

A project manager is managing a national book fair. Early in the planning phase, they identified some low-impact risks. What should the project manager do next?

    A. Ignore the risks since their impact is fairly low

    B. Add the risks to the risk register and keep monitoring them

    C. Develop a detailed risk response

    D. Report the risks to the fair sponsor(s)

Question 125

Maria is supervising three projects within her organization: two are of a similar type, while the third is entirely different. What is Maria's role in the organization?

    A. Project coordinator

    B. Project manager

    C. Program manager

    D. Portfolio manager

Question 126

Which of the following is an example of an information radiator?

    A. Prototype

    B. Milestone

    C. Kanban board

    D. Brainstorming

Question 127

Since leadership is crucial for project success, a project manager joins a training program to learn how to become a good leader. Which of the following activities should the project manager learn to apply in order to become the leader they aspire to be?

A. Guiding, motivating, and directing the project team

B. Improving their project's performance

C. Learning more about the specific domain of their project to be able to technically support the project team

D. Learning more about project management by obtaining a PMP certification

Question 128

A project manager has been requested to present the roles and responsibilities of their team members during the next meeting with the senior management. Which of the following should the project manager bring to the meeting?

A. Resource Histogram

B. Hierarchy Chart

C. RACI Chart

D. Gantt Chart

Question 129

__ is the float of activities on the critical path.

A. 0

B. 1

C. 2

D. It depends on the dependencies and duration of each activity

Question 130

A project manager is managing a project using the Scrum framework. The project manager receives a call from the product owner asking for a meeting with the team to discuss the possible approaches to implement user stories and make some initial size estimations. What type of meeting is the product owner referring to?

A. Sprint planning

B. Story mapping

C. Backlog refinement

D. Brainstorming

Question 131

A project manager works for a mobile app development company. One of his latest projects involves the creation of an exercise app that syncs with another nutrition app to combine and analyze the data. As a result of a recent regulatory change, the project team is working on refining the backlog. The process of backlog refinement involves:

A. The identification of the work items to be accomplished during the next sprint

B. A board to keep track of the product and sprint backlogs

C. A prioritized list of product requirements which is maintained by the project team

D. The gradual development of product specifications to meet the needs of the product owner

Question 132

A project manager is leading a team of 6 members in an open-space work environment. While working on an offer, the potential client called the project manager to ask for the cost estimate. The project manager informed them that it is around $600,000. A team member immediately corrected the project manager by saying "it's actually around $700,000". The project manager didn't even notice that the team member was overhearing the discussion. What kind of communication is being used here?

A. Open space communication

B. Distracting communication

C. Indirect communication

D. Osmotic communication

Question 133

A project manager is assigned to a university complex project that consists of designing and producing 200 wayfinding and directional signs. These signs will be placed and installed near doors, exits, offices, elevators, etc. by another company. After getting the client's approval that the project scope is met, the project manager delivers the signs to the installation company. The latter asks the project manager to help them with the signs' installation. What should the project manager do?

A. Submit a change request to assist with the signs' installation

B. Do a favor for the installation company and help them out

C. Create a new separate project charter for the signs installation support to make it clear that it's not part of the initial project

D. Do nothing since the project scope has been officially fulfilled and approved by the client

Question 134

One month into execution, a project's cost variance reached $0.90. What is the project's status?

A. The project is under budget

B. The project is over budget

C. The project will end up costing more than initially forecasted

D. The project will end up costing less than initially forecasted

Question 135

To avoid the frustration of wasted time and resources, a project manager relies on the project management plan before the project gets off the ground. Which of the following statements is true regarding the project management plan?

A. It identifies and authorizes the Project Manager to launch the project

B. It is a detailed project schedule defining the tasks and their dependencies, as well as key milestones

C. It is a formal document that defines how the project will be managed

D. It is part of the "Executing" process group

Question 136

An organization decides to develop an innovative system to control the quality of its products. The project manager assigned to the project opted for an Agile approach. Why did the project manager make this choice?

A. To avoid change requests as much as possible

B. To avoid scope creep as much as possible

C. To get feedback as early as possible

D. To complete the project as early as possible

Question 137

8 tasks of an Agile project release have the following story points: 3, 2, 5, 5, 8, 1, 3, 5. Given that the team's velocity is 10, how many iterations will they need to complete all of the 8 tasks?

A. 3

B. 4

C. 5

D. 7

Question 138

While examining their project progress, a project manager finds out that the schedule variance is $0.00. Which of the following statements is true about this project?

A. The project's CPI equals 1
B. The project's EV equals its PV
C. The project's cost variance is $0.00 too
D. The project's EAC equals its BAC

Question 139

A project manager is assigned to a network upgrade project. After the project scope approval, the Work Breakdown Structure (WBS) can now be created. Who is in charge of creating the WBS?

A. The project sponsor
B. The project manager
C. The project team
D. The product owner

Question 140

This is a project manager's first time leading an agile project. Knowing that they opted for the Scrum framework, which of the following describes the project team?

A. The team size ranges from three to nine members
B. All of the team members have a technical background
C. All of the team members are I-shaped
D. All of the team members are dependent on the Scrum master

Question 141

A project manager is in the phase of identifying and evaluating the risks of a construction project. One of the identified risks is so complex and ambiguous that the project manager decides to transfer it to the program manager so the latter can make the appropriate decision. How did the project manager respond to the risk?

A. Transfer

B. Mitigate

C. Escalate

D. Avoid

Question 142

A project manager is acquiring a team for a new project. A candidate for a particular position assures the project manager that he would be a great asset to the project team. The candidate adds that in case the project manager hires him, he would give the latter any project bonus he might receive. What should the project manager do?

A. Consider the candidate's statement a joke

B. End the job interview straightaway

C. Reject the candidate's job application

D. Accept the candidate's offer and hire him

Question 143

Which of the following statements about Risk Management is the most accurate?

A. Identified risks should be included in the risk register

B. Identified risks should be included in the Risk Management Plan

C. A risk that cannot be mitigated must be avoided

D. A risk that cannot be avoided must be mitigated

Question 144

A project manager was recently hired by an organization. In their previous position, the project manager used to have wide-ranging authority. Wondering if things will be different for them in the new organization, the project manager asked their mentor what type of organization it is. Which of the following options is not an organizational structure type?

A. Projectized

B. Matrix

C. Functional

D. Technical

Question 145

A project manager is managing a hostel redevelopment project. During a status meeting, one stakeholder asked the project manager why wallpaper was chosen over paint. Since the project manager had only joined the project during the execution phase, they were unable to answer the question. What should the project manager do? (Select two)

A. Inquire whether any other meeting attendees could answer the stakeholder's question

B. Change the subject to avoid responding

C. Confess that they don't know the answer, claiming that the question was irrelevant to the meeting's topic

D. Admit that they don't know the answer and promise to get back to the stakeholder after checking with the project team

Question 146

Match the following techniques with the corresponding description in the table below:
Brainstorming - Benchmarking - Focus group - Nominal group

Technique	Description
A. ------------	Interactive group discussion facilitated by a moderator
B. ------------	Group discussion to quickly generate a large number of ideas
C. ------------	Group discussion to produce ideas and prioritize them through voting
D. ------------	Comparison of ideas, products, processes, practices, etc.

Question 147

A project manager signs a contract worth millions of dollars to manage a 4-month international sports event. During the planning phase, the project manager discovers a serious threat to the project; one of their contractors might declare bankruptcy. If that happens, the project will be delayed for another two months. After giving it some thought, the project manager decides to contact another contractor who can supply the necessary materials. This is an example of:

A. Contract breach

B. Risk Transfer

C. Risk Acceptance

D. Risk Mitigation

Question 148

The project team includes the following members:

- Member A: excited about the project and eager to put in more effort if required
- Member B: always exceeds expectations
- Member C: well-liked by the customer and is willing to put in more effort as needed
- Member D: consistently achieves the project's requirements

Who is the most valuable resource to the project?

A. Member A

B. Member B

C. Member C

D. Member D

Question 149

Which of the following options are conflict-resolution techniques? (Select three)

A. Smoothing

B. Forcing

C. Adjourning

D. Withdrawing

Question 150

A project manager is managing a web application project using the Agile approach. During the first sprint, the team completed 4 tasks of 3, 5, 8, and 2 story points respectively. They also finished half a 13-story points task. What is the velocity of the team?

A. 18

B. 24.5

C. 31

D. 13

Full Mock Exam 2 - Answers

Question 1 = B

Explanation: Iteration review meetings take place at the end of each iteration to allow the project team to obtain feedback from the product owner and concerned stakeholders on a regular basis.

Question 2 = B

Explanation: The product owner should let the team do their work and answer any questions they might have during the sprint. The product owner should not add more tasks. Facilitating and protecting the team from interruptions are among the scrum master's responsibilities. Plus, the sprint duration is determined at the beginning of the project and typically does not change. Furthermore, any work items that cannot be completed by the team during the sprint should be put back in the backlog and rescheduled for the upcoming sprints.

Question 3 = A

Explanation: As the PMI code of ethics indicates under the Fairness chapter, the project manager should disclose any potential or real conflict of interest to stakeholders (PMI Code of Ethics and Professional Conduct, page 5).

Question 4 = B

Explanation: The project is 50% complete, so in order to calculate its EV, the following formula must be applied: EV = (BAC x % complete). The project's BAC is calculated by adding up all of the PVs of the project phases:

BAC = $2,000 + $2,000 + $3,000 + $3,000 = $10,000.

Therefore, the project's EV = ($10,000 x %50) = $5,000.

Question 5 = A

Explanation: The project charter is the document that authorizes the project manager to launch the project execution (PMBOK 7th edition, page 184). It also includes a brief description of the project and its requirements. Both the scope statement and the project management plan contain a detailed version of these requirements.

Question 6

Explanation:

A. Inspects progress towards the sprint goal = Sprint execution

B. Presents the project's performance to the stakeholders = Sprint review

C. Discusses the improvements that can be applied in the upcoming sprints = Sprint retrospective

D. Provides estimates of the required effort to complete user stories = Sprint planning

Please note that in the real exam such a question usually comes in the form of "drag & drop".

Question 7 = B

Explanation: Flexibility is one of the most important aspects of the Agile approach; the scope of work can change in response to new requirements. An Agile, adaptive, or change-driven approach encourages collecting feedback from stakeholders on a regular basis. Unlike the predictive approach, the Agile approach doesn't involve a Change Control Board (CCB).

Question 8 = B

Explanation: The client establishes the project's requirements. After all, the project was issued by the client. The project manager is in charge of meeting requirements rather than their definition. Business analysts and marketers are stakeholders that could influence the project's scope, but the client has the final say.

Question 9 = C

Explanation: The previous project manager made the assumption that the project would not experience any procurement delays. The described situation is not a constraint. Plus, there isn't enough information to determine whether the scenario involves a schedule variance or a critical path activity.

Question 10 = D

Explanation: The Kanban method involves pulling work into the system only when the team is capable of handling it. The Kanban method prioritizes productivity and efficiency through its workflow approach. Unlike the Scrum team, a Kanban team does not have predefined roles.

Question 11 = B

Explanation: A Pareto Chart is a vertical bar chart that ranks defects in descending order according to their frequency of occurrence. The Pareto Chart helps the project team focus on the causes that create the highest number of defects. Pareto's Principle, aka Pareto's Law, states that a limited number of causes usually produce the majority of defects or problems, which is referred to as the "80/20 principle" or "80/20 rule". PERT is not a chart; it's an estimation technique that uses a "weighted" average estimate rather than a simple average ((Optimistic + 4 * Mean +Pessimistic) / 6).

Question 12 = D

Explanation: An Agile retrospective meeting takes place at the end of each iteration during which the team discusses what happened during the iteration and determines improvement areas for future iterations. The retrospective allows issues to be identified and discussed along with ideas for improvements. Retrospectives are a primary tool for managing project knowledge and developing the team through discussing what went well and what needs to be improved (PMBOK 7th edition, page 71).

Question 13 = B

Explanation: 20% of the project's Earned Value is completed: EV = % finished x BAC = $24,000. $40,000 is the project's planned value and not its earned value. The $20,000 is the actual cost. The available information is enough to be able to calculate the project's EV.

Question 14 = D

Explanation: In order to reduce misunderstandings when using written communication mediums, the project manager can rely on the 5 techniques or the 5Cs of written communication, which represent: Correct grammar and spelling, Concise expression and elimination of excess words, Clear purpose and expression directed to the needs of the reader, Coherent, logical flow of ideas, and Controlled flow of words and ideas. Tone variation is a verbal communication technique.

Question 15 = A

Explanation: A Definition of Done is a checklist of required criteria in order to consider a product ready for delivery (Agile Practice Guide, page 151). Functional requirements describe the product requirements, e.g., website menus, functionalities, services, etc. Fit for Use is when a product serves its purpose as it is usable in its current state.

Question 16 = A

Explanation: Saving an endangered species of rhinos from extinction is the only correct example of a project since it has a unique outcome and a limited time frame. Governments and NGOs usually lead this kind of project which can take years. However, activities occurring after the project is complete, such as routinely keeping track of the endangered species population, could be considered operations. Periodically cleaning the local park, cyclically producing shoes, or routinely preparing dinner are all examples of operations rather than projects.

Question 17 = C

Explanation: Agile frameworks are known for their frequent and straightforward communication where a project manager is continuously checking in with the team to accordingly decide what could be alternatively done to improve the work pace and boost the team's morale. Daily communication should not be confused with daily standup. Daily standup meetings are held by the agile team members who follow a scrum framework. The project manager or scrum master is not required to attend this meeting, but even if they do, the daily standup meeting should not be their only channel of communication with the team. Whether you adopt a predictive or an adaptive approach for your project, you have to use formal and informal communication according to the situation.

Question 18 = A

Explanation: The project took more time than it should have most likely because the project scope was not clearly defined. There is no indication in the described situation that the project should have been broken down into smaller sub-projects. The project team doesn't usually have the power to approve or disapprove change requests. Changes conducted on the project scope fall under the Change Control Board's (CCB) responsibility. The fact that the project has exceeded its allocated time means that the sponsor is still supporting the project, therefore the project should not be halted.

Question 19 = A

Explanation: The process of breaking down project deliverables means the creation of the project Work Breakdown Structure (WBS). The Organizational Breakdown Structure (OBS) represents a breakdown of the project's hierarchy. The resource breakdown structure includes the composition of the project team. Requirements documentation is a record of product requirements and the relevant information needed to manage those requirements.

Question 20 = B

Explanation: If the team maintains an average velocity of 20 story points per iteration, it would take 11 iterations to complete the remaining 205 story points. (205 story points / 20 story points = 10.25 iterations). Since the timebox of an iteration should not be changed, the project team will need 11 iterations to complete the rest of the work.

Question 21 = A

Explanation: In the Scrum framework, the sprint planning meeting should include the scrum master, product owner, and the whole scrum team. When needed, other stakeholders can be invited by the team to attend this meeting. During the sprint planning meeting, the product owner identifies the features with the highest priority. The team asks questions to get the necessary understanding to be able to turn high-level user stories into more detailed tasks.

Question 22 = C

Explanation: Velocity refers to a Scrum development team's rate of delivering business value. An agile team's velocity is calculated by simply adding up the estimates or story points of all the features, user stories, requirements, or tasks successfully delivered by all team members during an iteration.

Question 23 = D

Explanation: Smoothing means smoothing away the issue by minimizing its perceived scale. Postponing decision-making depicts withdrawal. Taking a decision based on a 3rd party's input (the experienced team member) represents forcing. Taking into account both parties' opinions is known as compromise.

Question 24 = D

Explanation: Change requests may be submitted by any stakeholder involved with the project. The project sponsor(s), stakeholders, and the project team are all considered project stakeholders, therefore, they can all make change requests. CCB membership, power level, or involvement in project execution should not be restrictions for someone to request changes.

Question 25 = C

Explanation: During the "Validate scope" process, deliverables are compared against the acceptance criteria and requirements in order to formally sign off the completed deliverables. "Control quality" and "Control scope" should be carried out before the "Validate scope" process. "Validate Scope" consists in formalizing the approval and acceptance of the completed project deliverables. The verified deliverables obtained upon conducting the "Control Quality" process are the input of the "Validate Scope" process. One of the outputs of the "Validate Scope" process is the accepted deliverables that were formally signed off and approved by the authorized stakeholder.

Question 26 = B

Explanation: In order to establish a proper connection with the audience and jury, the project manager should make eye contact. It is critical to maintain eye contact with the receiving part of the communication process. The project manager should confidently look at the audience, without focusing on one person. Instead, they should make a sweeping glance at the audience from the left to the right and from the front to the back of the room to try and hold the attention of each member of the audience.

Question 27 = D

Explanation: The unwillingness to deal with a conflict is referred to as withdrawing. This conflict resolution technique is acceptable when some time to cool off is needed in order to achieve a better understanding of the situation, or when the other party is unassailable or uncooperative (PMBOK 7th edition, page 169). The situation does not imply problem-solving since the project manager didn't point out the issue to the sponsor in order to find a solution. The project manager didn't smooth the conflict either since there was no discussion with the sponsor to diminish their differences. Information recording, taking notes, or documenting the situation is not a conflict resolution technique.

Question 28 = B

Explanation: Material shortage, technical difficulties, scheduling conflicts, etc. are problems that should be recorded in the issue log. An issue log allows stakeholders to record and monitor active issues and their status; who's assigned to follow up and resolve a particular issue, for instance.

Question 29 = B, C

Explanation: The purpose of creating the Work Breakdown Structure (WBS) is to both organize and visualize the project scope. This document organizes work into work packages and assigns each package a code of accounts. Besides, as a visual tool, the WBS helps the team check the overall work plan, see how the project should progress, and appropriately manage the project workflow. The WBS is developed after identifying the project requirements and defining its scope.

Question 30 = B

Explanation: Scrum teams use four main events: sprint planning, daily scrum, sprint review, and sprint retrospective.

Question 31 = B

Explanation: The burnup and burndown charts are created to identify the amount of workload achieved and how much remains to be completed (PMBOK 7th edition, page 188). In a burndown chart, the line goes downwards, while in a burnup chart, the line goes upwards, which in both cases illustrates the team's progress. When burndown or burnup charts reveal issues related to sprint progress, which can be due to both technical or non-technical reasons, a self-organizing team should take corrective actions. In their next retrospective meeting, the team needs to reflect on what happened and how to better handle issues in the future.

Question 32 = A

Explanation: The term "impediment" refers to problems and issues that stop the project team's progress. Impediments should be constantly and regularly identified as they can hinder a project's completion. Identifying, tracking, and helping remove impediments is one of the main responsibilities of the Project Manager or Scrum Master. Often, team members are able to remove their own impediments, as in the case of technical issues or risks. However, some impediments involving external issues or risks can be beyond the team's ability to remove them. In this case, opting for support from outside of the Team is needed to overcome impediments.

Question 33 = D

Explanation: Since it's less than one, a 0.91 CPI indicates that the project is over budget; meaning that the project spent more money than expected. There is no evidence that the project is behind or ahead of schedule.

Question 34 = C, D

Explanation: When managing an Agile project, risk identification occurs in all types of planning meetings, such as daily stand-ups, release meetings, iteration reviews, and retrospectives. The project team analyzes and addresses risks during planning meetings through qualitative analysis rather than quantitative analysis. In Agile projects, the project team owns Risk management, while the project manager is only responsible for facilitating the process.

Question 35 = C

Explanation: Team velocity, i.e., the sum of story points' sizes of the completed features in the current iteration, allows the team to plan its next iteration more accurately by taking into consideration their historical performance (Agile Practice Guide, page 64).

Question 36 = B

Explanation: During the daily standup, the scrum master listens to the team members for any faced impediments and provides support in case of need. It's recommended that the standup meeting is facilitated by any team member rather than the project manager to ensure it does not turn into a status meeting. Ideally, it is a time for the team to self-organize and make commitments to each other (Agile Practice Guide, page 54).

Question 37 = D

Explanation: It's not enough to complete a project on time and under budget. You need to deliver value by creating a suitable product for your stakeholders' needs. Customer satisfaction is about making sure that the people who are paying for the end product are happy with what they ultimately get. Conformance to requirements and usability of deliverables is the basis of customer satisfaction as they allow you to measure how well your product meets expectations.

Question 38 = B

Explanation: Historical data is the most useful when it comes to validating project assumptions. Constraints can't help the project team confirm an assumption. Organizational rules help establish the project parameters rather than validate assumptions. Team members' recollections or memories are not reliable since they're not recorded. The team can use past experiences, documentation, proof, feedback, and any previously completed projects or project work as historical data to verify if a particular assumption is correct or realistic.

Question 39 = C

Explanation: Attempting to produce deliverables of a higher quality than required to exhaust the allocated budget and satisfy the project client is known as gold plating. The described scenario depicts poor project and cost management. The Integrated change control process consists of reviewing, approving or rejecting, and managing change requests, which is not the case here. Budget compliance is an irrelevant concept used in the information security domain.

Question 40 = D

Explanation: Unlike the burnup chart which shows the completed work, a burndown chart is a graphical depiction of the work that still needs to be completed (PMBOK 7th edition, pages 108).

Question 41 = A

Explanation: Bids, tenders, quotes, and proposals intersect with each other. Bids or tenders are used when the project is large and the scope of work is clear. Quotes, however, are mainly used to provide the price of particular products or services.

Question 42 = B

Explanation: The sum of all tasks is 32 story points. Therefore, after calculation, you'll find that it will take 3.2 iterations for the team to complete the tasks of the given release:

(32 story points / 10 story points = 3.2 iterations)

However, since the timebox of an iteration should not be changed, 4 iterations are needed to complete the release tasks.

Question 43 = A

Explanation: A Cost Performance Index (CPI) of less than 1 means that the project is over budget. A CPI of 1 indicates that the project is on budget. A 0.99 SPI means that the project can be considered on schedule (SPI = 1 means that the project is perfectly on schedule). Requirements can dictate that the project's final budget should be $100,000 (Budget At Completion, BAC), which is considered a constraint rather than an issue.

Question 44 = C

Explanation: A Minimum Viable Product (MVP) is a prototype with just enough features to be presented to early users, who can then provide feedback for future product development (PMBOK 7th edition, page 243). An MVP could be subject to many changes and subsequent prototypes, thus it can't be considered a pre-production version. A sample is a small part of a product intended to demonstrate the characteristics of the whole product. Product increment involves a workable increment delivered at the end of each iteration.

Question 45 = C

Explanation: The "Identify stakeholders" process should take place either before or concurrently while creating and approving the project charter. Stakeholders' identification should be carried out as many times as needed. However, it should always be executed at the beginning of each project phase and whenever a significant change occurs on both the project and the organization level. Since the first phase was complete, this means the scope has already been validated. Risks, on the other hand, are identified early on in the project. Nonetheless, you should keep monitoring and identifying new risks throughout the project execution. Likewise, activities are determined during the planning stage of each project phase, unless you're employing the rolling wave technique or adopting other life cycles rather than the traditional approach, which is not the case in this situation.

Question 46 = B

Explanation: An internal project is a project in which the customer is a person or department within your company. An external project, however, is a project in which the customer is an external party, whether it is a person or an organization. The customer or the client is the person, department, or organization that is supporting the project's development financially. The end-user of a product is not necessarily the project client or customer. Some corporations focus almost entirely on internal projects. Internet and software companies, for instance, primarily create internal projects in which they are their own client and their end-user is the general public (Fundamentals of Technology Project Management by Colleen Garton, Erika McCulloch, page 84). There is no indication in the question that the project is large or that it adheres to a traditional or agile approach.

Question 47 = C

Explanation: The project manager should schedule a meeting with the concerned stakeholders to present the project, discuss and establish ground rules, ensure their involvement and identify any personal or organizational issues. The project manager can overcome stakeholder resistance by simply listening to their concerns. The purpose is to see things from their perspective. The project manager should understand what drives and motivates the stakeholder in order to establish common ground and understand the reason behind such resistance.

Question 48 = C

Explanation: A defined budget is a project limitation i.e. a constraint. A predetermined project budget sets the maximum amount of money that the project manager is allowed to spend on a particular project, representing a limiting factor (constraint) for the project that can impact its quality, delivery, and overall success.

Question 49 = B

Explanation: Anonymously gathering the input of subject matter experts depicts the use of the Delphi technique, also known as the Delphi method or Delphi forecasting. This technique can be performed by sending an anonymous questionnaire or poll to gather advice from each expert, followed by a group discussion. Expert Judgment is too generic as an answer since it can employ several techniques such as the Delphi technique, focus groups, etc. Brainstorming is used to generate and analyze ideas in an interactive group environment. Focus groups bring together prequalified stakeholders and subject matter experts to openly and interactively discuss their expectations and attitudes about a proposed product, service, or result.

Question 50 = B

Explanation: the daily standup is a meeting held by members of the project team. This meeting brings the team together for a status update, to ensure that everyone is on the same page and has insight into what is going on, whether it's good or bad. Such a meeting usually takes up to 15 minutes during which every team member is asked three questions: What did you do yesterday that helped your team meet the Sprint goal? What will you do today to help your team meet the Sprint goal? And, Did you face any impediments that prevented you or your team from meeting the Sprint goal? (PMBOK 7th edition, page 179)

Question 51 = C

Explanation: The right step consists in understanding why the feature was not accepted in the first place, then moving on to making the required updates. After that, the feature can be moved back to the backlog for reprioritization.

Deleting the user story is not a rational choice since the feature has already been developed, which implies that it brings added value to the product.

Question 52 = B

Explanation: A Project Kick-Off Meeting is considered the formal announcement of the project approval for execution. This meeting takes place at the beginning of the project, once the plan and the project itself get approved but before executing or starting any work (PMBOK 7th edition, page 179). The Project Kick-Off Meeting is usually attended by the sponsor, other managers, the project team, as well as contractors and vendors (Effective Project Management Traditional, Agile, Extreme, Hybrid by Robert K. Wysocki Pages 272, 273). The sprint planning meeting can't be the correct answer for the given situation because the sponsor, stakeholders, and key contractors do not usually attend this meeting. The status meeting, on the other hand, is used to track project progress, when execution has already started. And finally, the scoping meeting is used to define the deliverables of the project, which in this case, should have already taken place since the tournament has been planned and approved for execution as mentioned.

Question 53 = B

Explanation: The sponsor's role entails providing the project manager with the required tools and resources to carry out their work. The sponsor does not take part in managing the project, nor do they get involved in team members' assignments. In a functional environment, the project manager has very limited power, therefore they can't have the freedom to make all decisions in this type of environment.

Question 54 = D
Explanation: In an iteration-based agile project, the product owner works with the team to refine the backlog and prepare user stories for the next iterations throughout one or multiple sessions, in the middle of the iteration (Agile Practice Guide, page 67).

Question 55 = D
Explanation: Any change to the project management plan should go through the organization's change control process by issuing a change request.

Question 56 = A
Explanation: The compromise approach to conflict resolution is characterized by searching for solutions that bring a certain level of satisfaction to all parties involved in order to temporarily or partially resolve the conflict (PMBOK 7th edition, page 168). In the question, a temporary solution was suggested to ensure some degree of satisfaction for both the project manager and the functional manager (a lose-lose situation). On the other hand,

smoothing emphasizes areas of agreement rather than areas of difference, leading to a yield-lose situation.

Question 57 = B, D

Explanation: The meeting probably does not have either a clear agenda or a facilitator. An agenda organizes and structures a meeting's discussions, while a facilitator ensures that the agenda is being followed and respected. Minutes of Meeting, aka MoM, is a summary of what happened during a meeting. MoM serves as a written record for future reference, thus they cannot be what caused this meeting to be chaotic. The meeting already has an objective; concluding a procurement in the negotiation phase. But, since no one is assigned to facilitate the meeting, it's probable that the objective was not appropriately communicated to all attendees in the first place, resulting in the described chaos.

Question 58 = C

Explanation: The previous project manager made the assumption that the project would not experience any procurement delays. The described situation is not a constraint. Plus, there isn't enough information to determine whether the scenario involves a schedule variance or a critical path activity.

Question 59 = A

Explanation: The stakeholders can submit a change request that can be recorded, evaluated, and either approved or rejected by the Change Control Board (CCB). As long as the change management process is followed, the project scope can be changed. The project sponsor could be part of the CCB which will be taking the decision concerning the stakeholders' change request. Therefore, it's not appropriate for the project manager to escalate the situation to the project sponsor.

Question 60 = B

Explanation: The project manager is identifying stakeholders and analyzing their level of influence. Although the project has been active for two months, it is recommended to perform this activity on a regular basis, especially when the project gets into a new phase.

Question 61 = A

Explanation: The project is behind schedule and under budget. You can calculate the Schedule Performance Index (SPI) by dividing Earned Value (EV) by Planned Value (PV): SPI = EV / PV. If SPI > 1, then the project is ahead of schedule. If SPI < 1, then the project is behind schedule. The Cost Performance Index (CPI) is calculated by dividing Earned Value (EV) by Actual Cost (AC): CPI = EV / AC. If the CPI is > 1, then the project is under budget. If it is < 1, then the project is over budget.

Question 62 = C

Explanation: A story point is a metric used to estimate the difficulty of carrying out a given user story in an agile project. In other words, it is an abstract measure of the effort required to implement a user story. A story point is simply a number that indicates the difficulty level of the story. The difficulty varies depending on the complexities, risks, and efforts involved (PMBOK 7th edition, page 178).

Question 63 = A

Explanation: The cost increase should be tracked and communicated using a cost variance report. A formal representation of the cost increase is not necessary. A memo is not the appropriate means in this situation.

Question 64 = A

Explanation: The presentation outline represents a guide of the key elements covered in the presentation. It includes a comprehensive list that sums up what will be demonstrated to prospective customers, clients, or investors. It allows the pitcher to organize their thoughts, highlight fundamental points, and logically elucidate their ideas.

Question 65 = A

Explanation: According to the network diagram, the project is at high risk. With five critical paths and two near-critical paths, any delay of any activity belonging to these paths will result in the whole project's delay. Having more than one critical and near-critical path does not mean that the project requires more resources and an increase in the allocated budget. On the other hand, just because the project is at high risk of schedule delay does not mean it should be terminated.

Question 66 = C

Explanation: It is the responsibility of the Product Owner to maintain and refine the backlog. Upon receiving a new requirement, it should be added to the backlog and then prioritized for implementation. Any stakeholder, not just the product owner, can submit a request.

Question 67

Explanation:

A. Asynchronous communication: Increases flexibility and reduces pressure

B. Face-to-face communication: Builds connections and leads to more engagement

C. Written communication: Decreases ambiguity and ensures commitment

D. Virtual communication: Saves costs and limits interruptions

Question 68 = D

Explanation: Budget is the primary constraint in this project. Therefore, cost control is the most critical in this situation. Time and quality are always essential, however, budgetary constraints can impact project quality. Plus, in the described scenario, cost control seems to be more important for the project than scope control, since cost overruns can lead to considering the project a failure.

Question 69 = C

Explanation: The decision tree method can help the project manager choose the best option for their project. Decision trees are used to support the selection of the best course of action among several alternative possible options. The decision tree uses branches representing the different decisions or events and their associated costs and risks. A Pareto chart is mostly used to display and prioritize the various root causes of a problem or an error. Control charts display trends and sampling results and are used to determine whether a process is stable or has predictable performance. Trend analysis can predict future trends and outcomes based on historical data.

Question 70 = D

Explanation: Unlike parametric estimating, the analogous estimating technique uses expert judgment by comparing a particular activity to a similarly completed one on a previous project in order to determine its duration or cost. This means that the project manager should rely on expert feedback, i.e., completing a similar task in 14 hours.

Question 71 = D

Explanation: In Agile, a project manager (also known as scrum master, project team lead, or team coach) is responsible for removing impediments and ensuring that the cross-functional team performs and delivers the product as initially defined by the product owner (PMBOK 7th edition, page 73 & Agile Practice Guide, pages 40-41).

Question 72 = A, D

Explanation: Fishbowl windows and remote pairing are two techniques used to manage communication in remote teams. The project manager can create fishbowl windows by initiating long-lived video conferences, where team members join in at the beginning of the workday and leave at the end. Remote pairing, on the other hand, is when two or more people join an online event at a specific time to discuss and share screens when needed (Agile Practice Guide, page 46). Colocating the team is not always feasible due to many considerations such as cost, talent availability, regulations, etc. However, when possible, getting the team together in person on a regular basis is a good practice. Changing the project life cycle from hybrid to agile won't have any significant impact on communication if team members don't take any specific measures or techniques to improve the way they interact with each other.

Question 73 = B

Explanation: The Change Control System is a set of procedures that describes how modifications to the project deliverables and documentation are managed and controlled (PMBOK 7th edition, page 237). The Change Control Board (CCB) is responsible for reviewing, evaluating, approving, delaying, or rejecting changes to the project. Not every project has a change control board. The organizational process assets refer to plans, processes, guidelines, and knowledge repositories that are unique to and employed by the organization. The scope management plan, on the other hand, only explains the scope's definition, development, monitoring, control, and validation procedures.

Question 74 = A
Explanation: The Rolling wave method is used to address uncertainty by planning near-term work in detail while planning future tasks in a more broad manner (PMBOK Guide 7th edition, page 249). It's a form of progressive elaboration that sets up near-term plans and "rolls" into the longer term as more details become available. In this way, rolling wave planning allows work to progress in current and near-term deliverables while planning for potential work packages continues.

Question 75 = B
Explanation: In this case, the project is currently in the Collect Requirements process, which involves identifying and documenting the needs and requirements of stakeholders. Data gathering takes part in the Collect

Requirements process to obtain stakeholders' requirements. It puts in use tools and techniques like benchmarking, brainstorming, focus groups, interviews, questionnaires, and surveys.

Question 76 = A

Explanation: SMART is an acronym that stands for Specific, Meaningful, Achievable, Relevant, and Timely (PMBOK 7th edition, page 97). Each letter in SMART can have other alternatives, except the "S" which commonly refers to "Specific" or "Strategic and Specific".

Question 77 = A

Explanation: Stakeholders have the most influence and impact on a predictive project at its early stages. Stakeholder influence is mostly perceived in the early stages of the project. The project is flexible at this stage and can be changed and stakeholders generally take advantage of this. Once it starts to progress, the project takes on momentum and power of its own, thus, the cost of stopping it or altering its direction becomes very high. (Vogwell, D. (2003). Stakeholder management)

Question 78 = B

Explanation: Currency fluctuations can be handled using a Fixed Price with Economic Price Adjustment (FP-EPA) contract. This type of contract allows the adjustment of the fixed price or rate of the contract. The buyer and seller agree on pre-defined criteria for this adjustment. This is often used for long-term projects that can span multiple years to adapt to market uncertainties and changes. The criteria to adjust the fixed price are based on market conditions that are beyond the control of both the buyer and seller, including changes in the cost of labor and material, general inflation, and fluctuations in the currency market. In a Fixed Price Incentive Fee Contract (FPIF), the buyer pays the seller a defined amount plus an additional incentive if the seller meets defined performance criteria.

A Firm Fixed Price Contract (FFP) includes a fixed price that the buyer pays the seller regardless of the seller's costs. Fixed Price with Currency Adjustment is a made-up term.

Question 79 = A, C, D

Explanation: Overburdened teams tend to produce low-quality work results. They are also more likely to experience frustration, low morale, and poor performance as a result of being overworked, weary, and stressed. Conducting quality inspections more frequently can be a result of producing low-quality work: it's an indirect consequence rather than a direct one.

Question 80 = D

Explanation: Risk mitigation can imply prototype development in order to prevent the risk from scaling up. Creating a prototype will support the testing and through testing, you can generate the necessary data to probably even close the risk. To keep costs low, you can opt for partial prototypes for the specific portions of the process that involve the risk.

Question 81 = C

Explanation: A user story is a brief description of deliverable value for a specific user (PMBOK 7th edition, page 192). A user story is not a narrative story about users; it is a small, granular work unit.

Question 82 = A

Explanation: This situation could have been avoided if the project manager had used formal communication when discussing and approving changes to the contract terms. A phone call is considered informal communication, which means that any decisions made over the phone mainly rely on mutual trust since there is no written record of the discussion or any ensuing decisions. Formal communication, on the other hand, provides a record of any terms, conditions, dates, etc. that have been discussed and approved, binding both parties to comply with any decisions made. In this scenario, the project manager should have used a formal communication channel, such as emails, to keep a formal record of the contract changes requested and approved by the client.

Question 83 = B

Explanation: As soon as a change gets approved, the project manager must update the time, cost, and scope baselines to reflect the impact of the change on all project aspects. A change control system represents a description of the way changes to the project scope should be managed. Actual changes are not part of the change control system. Each change gets through review as well as risk assessment by the Change Control Board (CCB) before getting approved or rejected.

Question 84 = C

Explanation: Historical information can be helpful when developing analogous estimates or parametric estimates. Analogous estimating is usually less time-consuming and less costly than other techniques, such as bottom-up estimating, but it also tends to be less accurate.

Question 85

Explanation:

- Task A is not yet complete: Data. Work performance data is the raw measurements and observations made during project execution (PMBOK 6th edition, page 26).
- Task B is not accepted because of a security issue: Information. When data is analyzed, it becomes information.

- Task C had a huge impact on the burndown chart: Report. Examining the whole picture in a burndown chart is a form of reporting.
- Task D is added to the product backlog based on customer feedback: Practice. The activity of creating, refining, estimating, and prioritizing product backlog items is one of the agile practices.

Please note that in the real exam such a question usually comes in the form of "matching".

Question 86 = A

Explanation: Scope Baseline is the approved version of a scope statement, work breakdown structure (WBS), and its associated WBS dictionary (PMBOK 7th edition, page 188).

Question 87 = C

Explanation: The first thing the project manager should do is listen to the customer, take note of the reasons behind their dissatisfaction, and verify the deliverables. Once this is done, the project manager will be equipped with all of the needed information to make the best decision. If they realize that it's just a misunderstanding or the customer is missing some details regarding the project deliverables, then they can simply use their soft skills to explain and convince them that the deliverables are good. However, if the deliverables do not meet specifications or require improvement, then they should plan to implement changes in the upcoming iterations according to the priorities set by the customer. Since the project is hybrid, the project manager may also need to ask the customer to submit a change request if out-of-scope work is requested.

Question 88 = C

Explanation: The Triple Bottom Line (TBL) is a sustainability framework for evaluating a company's bottom line from the perspectives of profit, people, and the planet (PMBOK 7th edition, page 252). This concept implies that companies should commit to measuring their social and environmental impact, in addition to their financial performance, rather than solely focusing on generating profit.

Question 89 = C

Explanation: Before taking any corrective measures, the project manager should determine the underlying cause of the problem. If it turns out that the concerned team member is overallocated, it might be better to assign some of their work to other writers. Regardless of their slow work pace, the concerned team member is doing a great job. Therefore, removing them from the project can have a negative impact on the quality of the deliverables. Assigning them to non-critical tasks can have a bad impact on their motivation, plus it does not resolve the main problem, i.e. their slow work pace.

Question 90 = A

Explanation: Phase reviews, aka phase gates, phase exits, phase entrances, kill points, and stage gates, is a formal review of the project to evaluate its status. The results are documented and presented to the concerned stakeholders or the sponsor in order to get their approval to proceed to the next phase in the project lifecycle. It's called "Kill point" because when your board determines that your project hasn't achieved its objectives to date, they may decide to stop it (PMBOK 7th edition, page 244).

Question 91 = C

Explanation: The project team is expected to deliver shippable product features by the end of each iteration. During the Iteration Review meeting, the project team demonstrates their work to the product owner and concerned stakeholders, in order to get feedback and approval (PMBOK 7th edition, page 179).

Question 92 = C

Explanation: The project manager should recommend using Spike. As a research story, a spike represents a time-boxed effort that is dedicated to learning, architecture & design, prototypes, etc. to better understand critical technical or functional details and thus make accurate estimations. Progressive elaboration can be a solution if the used technology could be understood over time. But, since the user stories are going to be implemented during the subsequent iteration, then progressive elaboration is not feasible in this scenario. Refactoring is a technique for enhancing product quality. A value stream is used to determine which actions bring more value to customers.

Question 93 = C

Explanation: The contract comprises all of the other mentioned documents. Any changes to any of the predetermined contract terms between the subcontractor and the project manager, including the defined scope of work, should be addressed in the contract. The scope only reflects the change in the workload but it does not address how this change will impact other aspects (Fee increase, change of completion date, etc.). The procurement management plan is used to define the process of what, when, and how to acquire material or services from third parties. Yet, it doesn't define the contractual engagement with each of them. The change control system doesn't also define the relationship between the vendor and the project.

Question 94 = B

Explanation: The retrospective meeting is the right meeting to reflect on what happened during the sprint and how to improve the implemented processes. Therefore, rather than discussing how to improve future work efficiency, the meeting facilitator should steer back the discussion to only focus on the demonstrated feature and get the product owner's feedback on what has been produced. This being said, if the documentation needs improvement, team members should create a technical task for it and demonstrate its importance to the product owner during Sprint Planning.

Question 95 = C

Explanation: The best course of action for the project manager to handle unsupportive stakeholders is to create an efficient communication plan as well as a stakeholder engagement plan. As a project manager, you can't disregard or ignore any stakeholders regardless of their attitude towards your project. If anything, you should give more attention and put more effort into engaging unsupportive ones in case they have a key role or big influence on your project. An efficient communication management plan and stakeholder engagement plan will help you identify these unsupportive stakeholders' level of interest and power and plan your communication and the way you're going to engage them accordingly, making it easier to ensure their collaboration and even possible to win their support. Refusing to manage the project doesn't mean the project will be canceled, thus it won't change the fact that certain stakeholders will still lose their jobs. Moreover, since the project was chosen for execution, it's intended to bring added value in spite of its downside for some involved stakeholders.

Question 96 = C

Explanation: It will take the project team 3.3 iterations to complete the backlog work items:

(100 story points / 30 story points = 3.3 iterations)

It would take 4 iterations to complete the work because the timebox of the iteration shouldn't be changed. Since the question specifically asks how many weeks are needed for completing work, then 8 weeks is the right answer.

Question 97 = C

Explanation: While the project sponsor and eventually c-suite executives are accountable for the project, it is the project manager who assumes responsibility for achieving the project's objectives and overall success.

Question 98 = C

Explanation: Source Selection Criteria is a valuable tool for choosing a qualified seller from a short-list of potential candidates. This method can help the buyer ensure that the selected seller will offer the best quality for the products or services required.

Question 99 = C

Explanation: Training costs fall under the cost of conformance to quality. The cost of quality is too generic as an answer since it comprises both the Cost of Conformance and the Cost of non-conformance. The cost of nonconformance involves the cost of internal and external failure costs, which is not the case here. The described scenario does not mention that the training was conducted to comply with certain regulations.

Question 100 = D

Explanation: A mandatory dependency is also called a hard dependency or hard logic. For example, consider 2 activities A and B, if B has a mandatory dependency on A, it means action on B cannot be performed until action on A has been completed. A discretionary or soft logic dependency, on the other hand, is an optional or preferred dependency. External dependencies involve a relationship between project activities and non-project activities (PMBOK 7th edition, page 60).

Question 101 = A

Explanation: Velocity is the measurement of how much work is completed in each sprint. It is calculated by adding up the sizes of the completed items by the end of the sprint (Essential Scrum by Rubin, Kenneth S, page 119). The sprint backlog is a list of product backlog items pulled into a sprint, which may not be completed by the end of the sprint. Average velocity represents the average velocity of all the previous sprints. The forecasting velocity is used when the team is new to the Agile approach and has no historical data.

Question 102 = D

Explanation: RACI stands for Responsible, Accountable, Consulted, Inform. The RACI chart or matrix is an example of the Responsibility Assignment Matrix (RAM), which shows the relationship between activities and team members as it defines team members' roles and responsibilities. It's an efficient tool to make sure everyone is on the same page and understands what they are supposed to do.

Question 103 = A
Explanation: Integrated change control should be performed throughout the whole project, from start to finish. Integrated change control is the process of reviewing all change requests, approving or rejecting changes, and managing implemented changes. Therefore, it should not be limited to a specific process group or project phase.

Question 104 = A, B, D
Explanation: Lessons learned are sometimes morbidly referred to as "postmortems" (Fundamentals of Technology Project Management by Colleen Garton, Erika McCulloch, page 47). They are also known as retrospectives (PMBOK 7th edition, page 71). A status meeting is held to review the actual status as well as risks. Status meetings could be eventually followed by preventive or corrective actions, change requests, or lessons learned meetings.

Question 105 = B

Explanation: The issue log is the right document to note all issues and the way they were resolved (PMBOK 7th edition, page 185).

Question 106 = B

Explanation: Earned Value (EV) refers to the value of completed work, based on the approved budget assigned to that work. Cost Variance (CV) is the amount of budget deficit or surplus at a given point in time, expressed as the difference between the earned value and the Actual Cost (AC). Schedule Variance (SV) is a measure of schedule performance expressed as the difference between the earned value and the Planned Value (PV).

Question 107 = A

Explanation: Interactive communication is the most effective communication method to maintain and improve relationships with stakeholders. Interactive communication is a real-time, dynamic, two-way flow of information. On the other hand, push communication is delivered by the sender to the receiver. It is recommended when the sender sends information that does not need an immediate response from the receiver. Emails are an example of this type of communication. Pull communication, such as blog posts, is delivered from the sender to a large audience. Here information is available for people to access when they need to. Written communication is used to exchange formal or detailed information such as decisions, statistics, facts, etc.

Question 108 = A

Explanation: The project team made the assumption that all of the company's computers are compatible with the new operating system. Consequently, they planned the project based on this belief. But later on, they found out that their assumption is untrue. Assumptions should be logged during the project planning phase to take into consideration when creating the project plan, and that's what the team most probably did. Therefore, the issue is not a result of poor planning. Since it wasn't discovered during the project execution, the encountered issue wasn't identified as a risk. The purpose of the project is to implement the new version of the operating system, so it cannot be considered a constraint. Yet, the hardware characteristics of the company's computers are a constraint since they can hinder the project's success.

Question 109 = B

Explanation: The status meeting is a scheduled meeting that is held on a regular basis to monitor the project's progress. The quality review meeting, as the name suggests, is meant to tackle everything related to the project quality including any issues or possible improvements. The kick-off meeting is not a recurrent event; it's a one-time meeting that is usually held at the end of the project planning phase and the beginning of its execution phase to officially announce its start. Standup meetings are short, daily meetings attended by the project team to discuss what was achieved on the previous day, what issues were faced, and what is planned for the current day; they're not meant for discussing the project's overall progress.

Question 110 = A

Explanation: Douglas McGregor defined two models of worker behavior: Theory X and Theory Y.

The new manager exhibits the traits of Theory X managers, who believe that the majority of people dislike work, lack motivation, and are in constant need of supervision. Theory X managers adopt an authoritarian style to make their teams work (PMBOK 7th edition, page 160).

Question 111 = D

Explanation: Sprint Retrospective is a process-oriented meeting that is held at the end of each iteration. Its purpose is to explicitly reflect on the most significant events that have occurred during the iteration in order to make decisions on how to improve processes during the next iteration. Sprint review or demonstration, on the other hand, is a product-oriented meeting.

Question 112 = B

Explanation: A predefined template format is usually followed when developing user stories in order to indicate the user's class (their role), what this class wants to realize (their goal), and why they want to achieve this goal (the benefit) (Cohn 2004). Using the term "so that" in a user story is not mandatory if the purpose is clear enough to everyone; otherwise, "so that" should definitely be used when writing each user story (Essential Scrum by Rubin, Kenneth S, page 83).

Question 113 = B

Explanation: Even if there is no official archiving procedure in place, the company should still organize, index, and keep the data related to completed projects. Project records should be kept for future use, therefore they should not be discarded by the project manager. The client should not have access to the project archive since it might contain private confidential data.

Question 114 = A

Explanation: Collaboration is the best approach to resolving a conflict between members. This would involve an open dialogue where differing viewpoints and insights are exhibited and discussed to eventually reach a consensus and commit to the final decision (PMBOK 7th edition, page 168).

Question 115 = A

Explanation: The product backlog should be prioritized and organized based on the value that each item brings to the product and project. This value depends on several factors such as the item's complexity, criticality, and the risk associated with it. However, these factors are not the basis to determine the items' value. Each item's value is dictated by the Product Owner as well as the items' sequence in the product backlog.

Question 116 = D
Explanation: The correct value is "Responding to Change over Following a Plan". All of the other alternatives are the right values of the Agile Manifesto (Agile Practice Guide, page 8).

Question 117 = D
Explanation: The project manager's decision to stop construction work during July means that they're trying to avoid the risk rather than accept it. The project manager made the safe decision to stop all construction work during hurricane season to avoid the risk of financial loss or putting the project staff in danger. This risk response is suitable for threats of high priority, high probability of occurrence, and a considerable negative impact. The decision can not be to mitigate because mitigation implies that the project manager would attempt to reduce the threat's probability of occurrence and/or impact, which can't be done since they have no control over river floods, nor did they take any prior action to mitigate its damage if it does occur (PMBOK 7th edition, page 123).

Question 118 = D

Explanation: The situation describes a schedule constraint: the project needs to be completed within deadlines or else the company will be obliged to pay a daily fine.

Question 119 = A
Explanation: The process of breaking down project deliverables means the creation of the project Work Breakdown Structure (WBS). The Organizational Breakdown Structure (OBS) represents a breakdown of the project's hierarchy. The resource breakdown structure includes the composition of the project team. Requirements documentation is a record of product requirements and the relevant information needed to manage those requirements.

Question 120 = C
Explanation: Surveys and questionnaires are written sets of questions designed to quickly gather data from a large number of respondents who are usually geographically dispersed.

Question 121 = C, D
Explanation: This is an example of negative risk, therefore, the project manager should use either mitigation to minimize the impact of the risk or avoidance to completely eliminate the risk. The other two strategies, exploit and enhance, are positive risk response strategies (PMBOK 7th edition, pages 123, 125).

Question 122 = D

Explanation: The project manager should immediately inform the project sponsor of their findings. The PMI's Code of Ethics requires project managers to comply with all laws and regulations. Concealing such information can lead the organization to face legal issues. In the case of a predictive project, change requests can be only issued after setting the project baseline. In the described scenario, the project is neither authorized nor baselined since it's still in the project charter development phase.

Question 123 = A, B, C

Explanation: Memos, correspondences with subcontractors, and team members' contracts should all be included in the project's archive. Plus, the approved version of the project charter should be saved, while drafts could be discarded.

Question 124 = B

Explanation: Passive risk acceptance is an appropriate approach for low-impact risks. No proactive action is needed for passive acceptance other than periodically reviewing the threat to ensure that it is not significantly changing. On the other hand, active risk acceptance entails developing a detailed risk response or a contingency plan that would be implemented if the event occurred (PMBOK 7th edition, page 123).

Question 125 = D

Explanation: A portfolio manager coordinates and manages a group of related or non-related projects and programs.

Question 126 = C

Explanation: Information radiators, such as the Kanban board, are a visible display of up-to-date information concerning the team's work status. A milestone is a point or an event in the project that does not display status information. Brainstorming, on the other hand, is a data-gathering technique, whereas a prototype is a method of getting early feedback on requirements.

Question 127 = A

Explanation: Leadership skills involve the ability to guide, motivate, and direct a team. This skill set may also include negotiation, assertiveness, communication, critical thinking, problem-solving, and interpersonal skills (PMBOK 7th edition, pages 23-25). All other options can make the project manager a better manager rather than a better leader.

Question 128 = C

Explanation: RACI charts are a type of RAM chart, which show the project resources assigned to each work package and illustrate the connections between work packages or activities, and project team members. RACI stands for the different responsibility types: Responsible, Accountable, Consulted, and Informed. A RACI chart is used to ensure the clear assignment of roles and responsibilities within the team. The Resource Histogram provides information about resource usage over time. Hierarchy charts represent the organization's structure and illustrate the reporting relationships and chains of command within the organization. Gantt charts represent schedule information by listing activities, dates, and activity durations in a bar chart.

Question 129 = A

Explanation: On a critical path, the float of activities is zero. Float, often known as slack, is how long an activity can be delayed without causing the whole project to be delayed.

Question 130 = C

Explanation: Backlog refinement provides a chance for the product owner to discuss and address stories' requirements with the team. This can involve discussing requirements, potential approaches, and even estimations in order to end up with a clear vision of how to approach stories (PMBOK 7th edition, page 179).

Question 131 = D

Explanation: Backlog refinement refers to the progressive elaboration of project requirements where the Agile team collaboratively integrates reviews and updates with the sole purpose of satisfying the customer and product owner's needs (PMBOK 7th edition, page 235). The identification of the work items to be accomplished during the next sprint is carried out during the sprint planning. The backlog is a prioritized list of product requirements that is maintained by the team. An information radiator or a Kanban board helps to keep track of the product and sprint backlogs.

Question 132 = D

Explanation: Osmotic communication is when team members are in the same room and one person asks a question, others in the room can either contribute to the discussion or continue working (PMBOK 7th edition, page 243).

Question 133 = D

Explanation: Since they completed their project, which clearly consists of only designing, producing, and delivering the sign, and after getting the client's official approval of the project's deliverables, the project manager's mission is done. They're not part of the signs installation process therefore no further steps are required. The signs production project is completed therefore submitting a change request doesn't make sense. A company is already assigned to install the signs so there is no need to create a new project charter.

Question 134 = A

Explanation: The cost variance is the difference between the earned value (EV), i.e., the budgeted cost of work performed, and actual costs (AC). CV = EV – AC, If the variance is negative, the project is over budget and if the variance is positive, it is under budget. In the question, the cost variance is barely above 0, so the project is under budget. Since the variance is very close to 0 (90 cents), we can also consider the project to be on budget, but this was not included as an option. Cost variance helps to determine the project's current status, but it cannot determine or predict if the project will end up costing less or more than anticipated. For instance, when the CV is negative, the project manager could take preventive or corrective actions in order to steer the project back on track within the defined budget.

Question 135 = C

Explanation: A project management plan is a formal document that defines how a project is going to be carried out (PMBOK 7th edition, page 186). The project plan is created during the planning phase of the project life cycle, and it must be approved by stakeholders before the project can move on to execution. The project charter is a document that is meant to identify and authorize the Project Manager to start the project. The project management plan is created as part of the planning process group.

Question 136 = C

Explanation: Since it's based on short development iterations, Agile approaches allow for early and frequent feedback by delivering a working piece of the product at the end of each iteration to the customer. Since traditional projects can only obtain customer feedback at the end, it is often too late to incorporate the feedback or fix any issues at that stage, unlike Agile projects where new changes are welcomed and integrated into the product development process.

Question 137 = B

Explanation: The sum of all tasks is 32 story points. Therefore, after calculation, you'll find that it will take 3.2 iterations for the team to complete the tasks of the given release:

(32 story points / 10 story points = 3.2 iterations)

However, since the timebox of an iteration should not be changed, 4 iterations are needed to complete the release tasks.

Question 138 = B

Explanation: Schedule variance (SV) measures whether your project is on track by calculating its actual progress against expected progress to determine how ahead of or behind schedule the project work is. SV equals the difference between your project's earned value and planned value: SV = EV − PV. Therefore, an SV of $0.00 means that the project's EV equals its PV.

Question 139 = C

Explanation: The project team is responsible for carrying out the process of creating the project Work Breakdown Structure (WBS). Involving all stakeholders in the creation of the WBS can be both unrealistic and impractical since certain projects can include hundreds and even thousands of stakeholders. Plus, even if they were included, they would most likely lack the necessary skills to contribute to the creation of the WBS. The project manager is partially involved in the process and not responsible for performing it: they can only facilitate the WBS creation and provide the team with the needed help and direction.

Question 140 = A

Explanation: The typical size of an agile team ranges from three to nine members. Agile teams should be multidisciplinary (not necessarily have a technical background) and self-organizing (not dependent on the scrum master). Successful agile teams are made up of generalizing specialists/T-shaped members who have deep knowledge in one area and a broad ability in other areas. I-shaped, on the other hand, refers to a person with a profound knowledge of one area but has no interest or skill in other areas (Agile Practice Guide, page 42).

Question 141 = C

Explanation: In the described scenario, the project manager has escalated the risk to the program manager. When a threat is considered to be outside the project scope or when the appropriate response exceeds the project manager's authority, risk escalation is the suitable risk response strategy (PMBOK 7th edition, page 123). Risk escalation involves passing the risk to the right owner (the program manager in this case) to ensure that it is recognized, understood, and managed appropriately. Avoiding the risk means eliminating the threat or protecting the project from its impact. Risk mitigation implies decreasing the threat probability of occurrence and/or impact. And finally, transferring the risk entails shifting the threat ownership and responsibility to a third party which may involve payment of a risk premium to the third party assuming the threat.

Question 142 = C

Explanation: The best thing to do in this situation is to reject the candidate's job application. Apart from being unethical, offering or accepting a bribe is a huge violation of the PMI Code of Ethics. Even if the candidate was joking, this type of joke is inappropriate and an indication of his lack of professionalism. The project manager should avoid the fuss of ending the job interview straightaway and just reject the application later on.

Question 143 = A

Explanation: All identified risks should be added to the risk register. The risk register includes identified project risks, risk owners, agreed-upon risk responses, and specific implementation actions, as well as other details including control actions for assessing the effectiveness of response plans, signs of risk, residual and secondary risks, and a watch list of low-priority risks. Risk responses include: Avoid, Escalate, Transfer, Mitigate, and Accept (PMBOK 7th edition, page 123). A risk that cannot be mitigated or avoided could be escalated, transferred, or accepted.

Question 144 = D

Explanation: Technical is not an organizational structure. There are multiple types of organizational structures including functional or centralized, matrix, and projectized or project-oriented.

Question 145 = A, D

Explanation: It is important not to immediately respond to a difficult question without first taking some time to think about the answer. Repeating the question and asking for clarification will help the project manager take enough time to consider their response. It would be impolite to claim that the question was irrelevant to the meeting's topic. If the meeting is running late, the project manager could ask the stakeholder to discuss the topic after the meeting. Escaping the question is not a good idea either.

Question 146

Explanation:

A. Focus groups: involve an interactive group discussion facilitated by a moderator

B. Brainstorming: a group discussion to quickly generate a large number of ideas

C: Nominal group: a group discussion to produce ideas and prioritize them through voting

D: Benchmarking: involves a comparison of ideas, products, processes, practices, etc.

Question 147 = D

Explanation: The described situation depicts Risk Mitigation. The project manager did not cancel the contract because the contractor might go bankrupt. They did not breach the contract either by getting in touch with another supplier. They contacted a different vendor in order to keep their options open and have other alternatives in case the risk occurs. By doing this, the possibility of the project's delay is reduced.

Question 148 = D

Explanation: Team member D is the best project resource since they regularly meet project requirements. Even if Member A is excited and eager to put in more effort (Member A), exceeding expectations by spending additional time working on the project (Member B), or being well-liked by the customer (Member C), doesn't mean that these team members can meet the project criteria.

Question 149 = A, B, D

Explanation: Adjourning is one of the five stages of team development according to the Tuckman ladder. Conflict resolution techniques include withdrawal/avoiding, smoothing/accommodating, compromising, forcing, collaborating, and problem-solving/confronting (PMBOK 7th edition, page 169).

Question 150 = A

Explanation: Velocity is a measure of the amount of fully completed work in a sprint. Partially done tasks should not be counted. In this case, velocity = 3 + 5 + 8 + 2 = 18 points.

Full Mock Exam 2 - Result Sheet

Assign "1" point to each question answered correctly, and then count your points to get your final score.

1. ___	20. ___	39. ___	58. ___	77. ___	96. ___	115. ___	134. ___
2. ___	21. ___	40. ___	59. ___	78. ___	97. ___	116. ___	135. ___
3. ___	22. ___	41. ___	60. ___	79. ___	98. ___	117. ___	136. ___
4. ___	23. ___	42. ___	61. ___	80. ___	99. ___	118. ___	137. ___
5. ___	24. ___	43. ___	62. ___	81. ___	100. ___	119. ___	138. ___
6. ___	25. ___	44. ___	63. ___	82. ___	101. ___	120. ___	139. ___
7. ___	26. ___	45. ___	64. ___	83. ___	102. ___	121. ___	140. ___
8. ___	27. ___	46. ___	65. ___	84. ___	103. ___	122. ___	141. ___
9. ___	28. ___	47. ___	66. ___	85. ___	104. ___	123. ___	142. ___
10. ___	29. ___	48. ___	67. ___	86. ___	105. ___	124. ___	143. ___
11. ___	30. ___	49. ___	68. ___	87. ___	106. ___	125. ___	144. ___
12. ___	31. ___	50. ___	69. ___	88. ___	107. ___	126. ___	145. ___
13. ___	32. ___	51. ___	70. ___	89. ___	108. ___	127. ___	146. ___
14. ___	33. ___	52. ___	71. ___	90. ___	109. ___	128. ___	147. ___
15. ___	34. ___	53. ___	72. ___	91. ___	110. ___	129. ___	148. ___
16. ___	35. ___	54. ___	73. ___	92. ___	111. ___	130. ___	149. ___
17. ___	36. ___	55. ___	74. ___	93. ___	112. ___	131. ___	150. ___
18. ___	37. ___	56. ___	75. ___	94. ___	113. ___	132. ___	
19. ___	38. ___	57. ___	76. ___	95. ___	114. ___	133. ___	

Total:

N° of Correct Answers	% of Correct Answers
---------- / 150	----------

Did this book help you prepare for your CAPM certification exam? If so, I'd love to hear about it. Honest reviews help other readers find the right book for their needs.

About The Author

Yassine is a PMP® certified Instructor & Author with more than 10 years of experience in the IT field, moving up in his career through multiple positions like a Business Developer, Account manager, Functional consultant, Product owner, Office manager, up to being currently a Project manager.

Managing and leading both on-site and remote projects, in the public and private sectors, Yassine is passionate about helping and sharing his Project Management expertise and knowledge.

Relying on his academic background along with his real-life experience managing projects in Telecommunications, Retail, Financial Services, and more, Yassine aims to present practical rich content suitable for beginners as well as professionals in the PM field.

Yassine strongly believes in the practical methodology, offering easy to apply knowledge that he is certain about its efficiency considering that he practices what he preaches in his daily position as a Project Manager.

Made in the USA
Monee, IL
19 January 2023

25668488R00177